Decoding You

A beginner's guide to self-discovery through the Enneagram and Numerology

By

ARUN SHANKAR

First Edition

ardra
publishers
London, United Kingdom

Decoding You : A beginner's guide to self-discovery through the Enneagram and Numerology

By Arun Shankar

Copyright © 2023 by Arun Shankar

All rights reserved. No part of this publication may be reproduced, distributed, or transmitted in any form or by any means, including photocopying, recording, or other electronic or mechanical methods, without the prior written permission of the publisher, except in the case of brief quotations embodied in critical reviews and certain other non-commercial uses permitted by copyright law of each country.

All excerpts, quotes and references of any books, authors and illustrations are copyright of the respected authors and creators.

ISBN: 978-1-7395686-0-3

First Edition : September 2023

First Printing in 2023

Ardra Publications
London, United Kingdom
www.ardrapublications.co.uk

Jai Ganesh!

*To my beloved dad,
who I know would be extremely happy reading this in heaven.*

To Arya, my steadfast anchor.

To Arnav and Arnika, the compass guiding my journey.

To my Mom, brother and sister, completing my world.

The information provided in this book is intended for informational and educational purposes only. Neither the author nor the publisher assumes any responsibility or liability for the use or misuse of the material presented herein. Readers are advised to exercise their own judgment and consult relevant experts when necessary.

All references to public figures and celebrities in this book are made in an observational capacity and are based on publicly available information. These references are speculative interpretations and do not claim to reflect the actual thoughts, feelings, or experiences of the individuals mentioned. They are not intended to portray the individuals in any particular light and should not be considered as definitive representations of the persons involved.

Acknowledgements

A journey of a thousand miles begins with a single step, but it also requires the company of fellow travellers and guides who enrich the journey and make it memorable. Writing this book has been a transformative expedition for me, and I owe my deepest gratitude to a circle of invaluable souls who have been instrumental at various stages of its creation.

At the forefront of my gratitude stands my most beloved father, Shri Sankarankutty Nair, who now watches over me from the heavens. Your nurturing and life lessons fuel my constant quest for truth.

With a heart full of devotion, I also thank my celestial guides Ganesha, Krishna, and Manikanta, for being the torchbearers in my life, guiding me from darkness to light at every twist and turn.

My most beloved wife, Arya, you are the rock on which I stand. Your unwavering support and love have transformed challenges into stepping stones, enriching this odyssey in immeasurable ways. A pillar of love and understanding, my mother Anila Sankar deserves a special place in these acknowledgements. Alongside her are my cherished siblings, Dr. Akhil Sankar and Dr. Asha Sankar, who form an unbreakable support network that I know will endure for a lifetime.

A special acknowledgment to Shri. Madhu Unnithan, who has not only been a brother to me but also a mentor on this path towards the greater understanding. Your guidance has enriched my thoughts and work immeasurably. I also extend my thanks to Dr.Sreenath Karayatt for opening the intriguing doors of the Enneagram to me. Your expertise is what made this entire endeavour a reality.

I also wish to thank Enneagram pioneers like Don Richard Riso, Russ Hudson, Helen Palmer, Richard Rohr, Claudio Naranjo, Oscar Ichazo, and Beatrice Chestnut. Your ground-breaking work laid the very foundation of this book.

And finally, a collective bow of gratitude to Shri. Sudeesh Rajashekharan, Shri. C E Ajith Kumar, Shri. Ashok Rao, Shri. Rajiv R, and Shri. Praveen V. Each one of you has played a distinct part in the journey of this book, and for that, I remain deeply indebted.

*"Know thyself,
and the cosmos will mirror your essence"*

Hello, Dear Reader...

In the hustle and bustle of everyday life, we often forget to explore the deeper realms of our existence. I, too, was once wrapped up in my engineering work—analysing numbers, solving equations. But there's another part of me that's always been enthralled by the ancient wisdom that cultures across the world have to offer. Whether it's the Vedas from India or the Pythagorean teachings of the West, I've found these ancient texts to be more than mere stories—they are guides, offering alternative ways to view the world.

It was a course on the Enneagram by Dr. Sreenath Karayatt that ignited my interest in blending the mystical and the scientific. I began to see numbers and personality traits not just as independent entities, but as interconnected aspects of our lives. With the mentorship of Shri. Madhu, the idea for this book started to germinate. I realized that what I was learning could be of value to others as well. So, here it is—a book that aims to offer you the keys to unlocking deeper self-understanding.

This book isn't just a collection of words; think of it as an engaging conversation between you and me. We're going to delve deep. We're going to ask questions about what makes us who we are, and how numbers and personality types shape our lives. The book combines the spiritual wisdom of ancient India with modern-day psychology. It's a journey that will take you into the recesses of your soul, asking you to contemplate who you really are and what you're here for.

Our journey will unfold over the chapters that follow, each one like a new path in an unexplored forest. We'll dig into the Enneagram, a system that gives us insights into human behaviour. And we'll explore numerology, a practice that traces its roots back to ancient cultures. The book is like a bridge, linking two fascinating realms and helping you walk across.

So, welcome to this shared journey, an exploration where numbers meet souls, and where questions lead to more questions, but also to enlightenment. Let's turn the page and begin our voyage. You're not just a reader of this book; you're an active participant in its story.

Let's begin!

Table of Contents

The Hidden Passageways Of Life 1

The Enneagram 5

Learning Enneagram 17

The Enneagram Symbol 23

Inner Symphony Of Enneagram 39

Enneagram And Inter-Relationships 49

Embracing Redemption 55

A Journey Of Self-Discovery 63

Enneagram Types 71

Numerology 91

Chaldean Numerology 99

The Chaldean Numbers 111

Vedic Numerology 119

The Kaṭapayādi System 127

System Of Vedic Numerology 131

The Planets & Numbers 139

The Contrast 157

The Unfinished Symphony 167

Chapter One

The Hidden Passageways of Life

Ever wondered why some people seem to have it all figured out while the rest of us are left scratching our heads? Is there a hidden roadmap they've discovered? Well, the answer is both simple and complex—there's a treasure map, alright, but it's not hidden in some ancient cave. It's coded right within you. Imagine being the hero of your own life's adventure, like an Indiana Jones but of the spirit, armed with wisdom and guided by numbers.

Think of it this way: you're like an undiscovered manuscript filled with fascinating stories and life-changing secrets. But to unfold these pages, you've got to do more than just skim through. This takes us on a journey back in time, about 5,000 years back, to the period when the Vedas were written. These ancient texts gave us something astonishingly enduring—Vedic Numerology. It's not just counting or doing math; it's the universe's own language, one that's been there since the dawn of time.

Now, don't consider this some quick weekend retreat to 'find yourself'. Nah, this is the ultimate road trip of your life. You could be anywhere—in the middle of a bustling crowd or alone with your thoughts on a quiet beach—when an insight might strike you like a lightning bolt. That's the power of understanding your numbers or grasping the Enneagram frameworks; they're the signposts on your personal journey, your inner GPS. The thrilling part is, life turns into an unfolding mystery where you are both the detective and the enigma. Every revelation adds a new twist to your personal saga, opening up pathways you didn't even know existed. The closer you get to cracking the code of your own complexities, the more life opens up in ways you never expected—be it in relationships, career, or your personal growth.

But hold your horses! This isn't a 'solve it and it's done' kind of puzzle. Oh no, the more you dig, the more you discover—a labyrinth of questions, wonders, and yes, some inevitable challenges. It's the longest-running show with the most captivating plot, and you are the star.

So, ready to crack the first clue? Strap in for this never-ending saga where the script keeps changing but the hero—yes, that's you—remains at its thrilling heart. And you'll soon find that you're a much more riveting character than you ever gave yourself credit for. How's that for a gripping first chapter?

✳✳✳

Your journey through understanding human nature is like walking through an ancient, never-ending library. Each book is penned by philosophers, sages, and modern-day scientists who've handed down their wisdom for generations. They've filled the library with their teachings, from the metaphysical mantras of the Vedas to the psychological blueprints of Freud and Jung. But among these countless volumes, there's a special section—two guidebooks, if you will—that have an immediate, everyday impact: Enneagram and Vedic Numerology.

You can imagine the Enneagram as a handbook written by an expert trekker for a mountain expedition. This trekker knows every twist, turn, and slippery slope. The book tells you not only about your own hiking style—whether you speed ahead, take it easy, or like to stop and enjoy the view—but also how you interact with your fellow trekkers. Why do you react as you do when you're exhausted or when you hit a roadblock? The Enneagram provides the know-how to navigate these human terrains.

Next to it sits the guidebook of Numerology, seemingly scribbled by a sage who's spent years under the banyan tree in deep meditation. Even though we have a handful of different schools of numerology from the ancient civilizations, we will particularly look into the Chaldeans and the Indian Vedic numerologies in this book. It whispers to you that your birth numbers and name are like a cosmic QR code. They unveil your natural talents and your life's purpose, but they also give you practical advice.

Don't get me wrong; these aren't shortcuts to enlightenment or self-realization. Rather, think of them as handy tools in your daily life toolbox. Want to be a better leader at work? These can help. Trying to understand what makes your partner tick? These offer clues. From shaping your personal relationships to understanding societal dynamics, these are practical lanterns lighting up your path in an otherwise dark cave.

And just a word of caution – this book is just a first step towards all the topics we discover here. We give it to you as an appetizer before the seven-course meal which you have to have by continuing the spirit and quest for this knowledge. What I am trying to do here is just to show you a trailer of what you can achieve through these systems. Watching the show in its full is another bigger journey! The library of human understanding is expansive, and while many books offer grand theories, these particular guidebooks serve the immediate, concrete needs of your daily life. Will you pick them up and read them, or let them gather dust on the shelf? The next chapter, as they say, is yours to write. Are you ready?

Chapter Two

The Enneagram

The Enneagram isn't merely a fleeting trend that has caught the public's attention; it's a long-standing system that delves deep into human personality. The system's roots stretch far back, borrowing from various intellectual traditions—from the philosophical musings of ancient Greece, the spiritual wisdom of Egypt, and even the metaphysical insights from our own Indian subcontinent. This medley of influences showcases the Enneagram's universal appeal, proving that the quest for understanding human nature transcends time and space.

The name Enneagram comes from the Greek: *Ennea* is the Greek word for nine and *Gramma* means something that's drawn or written.

So, what makes this ancient system resonate with modern psychology? It's all about practicality. Once a guide for spiritual seekers, the Enneagram today has been adapted to the current era by visionaries like Claudio Naranjo, Don Richard Riso, and Russ Hudson. These modern torchbearers have repurposed it into a scientific tool, used for demystifying the often-baffling complexities of human behaviour. This transformation owes much to Oscar Ichazo, a man who acted as a conduit between the Enneagram's historic roots and its contemporary applications. Ichazo took this ancient wisdom and injected it with a dose of psychological relevance, rescuing it from the risk of becoming a historical footnote.

Now, this isn't a tool restricted to the chambers of psychologists or the pious corridors of spiritual gurus. Think of a classroom—a place where young minds are moulded. Teachers armed with the Enneagram can decode the different learning styles of their students. It turns the classroom from a monologue into a dialogue, from a one-size-fits-all model into a diverse but unified learning environment.

And what about families? Every parent knows that raising a child doesn't come with an instruction manual. But, with the Enneagram, it's almost as if you have a field guide to your child's ever-changing temperament and emotional needs. Understanding why your child behaves in a particular way can transform the parent-child relationship from a struggle into a journey of mutual discovery. The workplace is another battleground of contrasting personalities, where the Enneagram proves invaluable. This isn't just about resolving conflicts; it's about building a team that understands and complements each other's strengths and weaknesses. When a leader can match tasks to team members based on their inherent traits, the result is a harmonious, more productive workplace. The utility extends from the HR departments to the cubicles and even the boardrooms.

Now, let's extend our gaze to the realms of personal relationships. The counsellor's office, often seen as a last resort for distressed couples, becomes a space of revelation with the Enneagram. Through understanding one's partner's type, the dynamics of a relationship can change; conflicts can be navigated, and new pathways of understanding can be forged. It's like having a translator for emotional language, making each partner's needs and expectations more legible to the other.

The Enneagram has more to give. In the rapidly evolving field of education, certain forward-thinking institutions are incorporating it into their pedagogy. By understanding the Enneagram types of students, curriculum developers are beginning to tailor education in a more personalized manner. It's not just the subject matter that is considered; it's how each student will absorb and relate to the material. That's revolutionary. Remarkably, the Enneagram has also found its way into the legal system. Legal professionals, curious about human motivation and behaviour, have started to use it as a supplementary lens. It's not about proving innocence or guilt but about understanding the layers of human psychology that may influence actions. It provides a nuanced perspective that can be invaluable in complicated legal proceedings.

The Enneagram's spiritual roots should not be forgotten either. Numerous spiritual leaders and communities are embracing it as a means of personal development. It's becoming increasingly common to find Enneagram workshops being conducted in monasteries, churches, and spiritual retreats. This convergence of science and spirituality shows the system's adaptability and wide-reaching relevance. Another significant point is that the Enneagram is not static; it's an evolving framework. As more studies are conducted and more data analysed, expect to see some refinements. But the core will remain—the essential purpose of understanding human nature for improved coexistence will continue to be its focus.

So, the Enneagram is not just a system that has been passed down through the annals of history; it's a living, breathing framework that continues to adapt and find new applications. From classrooms and living rooms to corporate offices and legal chambers, it has proven to be an invaluable asset. With roots deeply planted in ancient wisdom and branches that reach out to grasp modern complexities, the Enneagram serves as an evolving guide for humanity. The Enneagram is not just a theoretical concept; it is a practical tool for anyone interested in understanding the intricate mosaic of human personality. With its multi-faceted applications and enduring relevance, it remains a robust and highly useful system for personal and societal well-being.

Ancient Beginnings and Early Influence

The Enneagram is an intriguing subject, not least because it sparks debates that stretch across time and space, connecting ancient civilizations like Greece and India to our present day. It's like a river whose source we're not quite sure of, but whose tributaries we recognize. Yet it's difficult to point exactly to where it all began, what blend of ideologies and philosophies gave rise to this intricate system that tries to decode the mysteries of human behaviour.

In ancient Greece, Pythagoras stands as a crucial link to the Enneagram. He is widely respected for his contributions to mathematics and geometry but also had a profound interest in spirituality. Pythagoras spent a significant amount of time in Heliopolis, Egypt. This city was a religious hub famous for the worship of the Ennead, a group of nine prominent deities in Egyptian mythology. During his stay, it's conceivable that he encountered the foundational ideas that would later shape the Enneagram. In addition to the Ennead, the concept of 'nine' holds special importance in Greece through the Nine Muses—the goddesses of the arts, literature, and science. Just as the Ennead covers a broad spectrum of life's facets, the Nine Muses encompass various domains of human creativity and knowledge.

Switching our focus to India, the land with rich Vedic traditions offers another lens to view the Enneagram. Vedic philosophy has a longstanding history with numerology, geometry, and astrology. Numbers in India are not just digits; they bear a philosophical and spiritual significance. This is particularly striking in Vedic astrology, where celestial positions are interpreted through complex geometric designs. The Indian practice of assigning greater meaning to numbers echoes with the Enneagram's categorization of human personalities.

Now, let's return to ancient Egypt to add another layer to our understanding. The Egyptians, mainly in Heliopolis, worshipped the Ennead, often called the Great Ennead, which is a collection of nine gods and goddesses who were highly respected in Egyptian folklore. These divine beings were mainly worshipped in the city of Heliopolis. Atum, the sun god, is at the apex of this pantheon, followed by his offspring Shu and Tefnut. The lineage continues with Shu and Tefnut's children, Geb and Nut, and further extends to their progeny—Osiris, Isis, Set, and Nephthys. Sometimes, Horus the Elder, a different version of the falcon deity and not to be confused with Osiris and Isis's son, is also included in the Ennead. Just like the nine Muses in Greece, the Ennead in Egypt represented a multi-faceted view of human experiences and emotions. It wouldn't be far-fetched to think that Egyptians might have considered this structure as a guide for navigating the maze-like complexities of human behaviour.

From Egypt, it made several stops, as if on a grand voyage—touching base with various religious and spiritual communities, each adding its hue to the Enneagram's already colourful canvas. It found its way into mystical Judaism, Christian doctrines, Islamic teachings, Taoist philosophy, Buddhist thoughts, and back to ancient Greek ideologies. Each belief system folded it into their teachings, enriching its structure and making it as diverse as it is today. So, if you think about it, the Enneagram isn't merely a tool or a system; it's more like a palimpsest written over centuries, where each community has left its indelible mark.

Let's bring in a more modern take. In his book "The Sacred Enneagram: Finding Your Unique Path to Spiritual Growth", Christopher Heuertz suggests that the Enneagram might have roots even beyond the Jewish and Christian narratives, expanding its sphere to a more universal, mystic realm. Here, Heuertz gives a nod to Beatrice Chesnut, who raises the point that the Enneagram's origins might be embedded in texts that are still to be discovered, places that are yet to be explored. Interestingly, Heuertz refers to Homer's "The Odyssey", where the hero Odysseus traverses through nine different lands, each teeming with unique challenges and characters. The correlation between these nine worlds and the Enneagram's nine types is too obvious to ignore. Could it be that the wisdom of the Enneagram is ageless, its principles universal? Heuertz seems to think so, arguing that the text was designed to steer its readers toward a profound journey of self-discovery. However, and this is where the plot thickens, not everyone is buying into this idea. Critics argue that the theories put forth by Heuertz and Chesnut are not grounded in extensive research. They caution against reading too much into ancient texts, pointing out the risk of projecting modern constructs onto them. Simply put, while it's tempting to view the Odyssey as a coded guidebook to understanding the Enneagram or the human psyche, we must tread carefully.

One word of caution before we close this topic — the Enneagram has had its share of dark days. There were periods when it was twisted to fit dubious belief systems, sometimes even being used for manipulative purposes. But today, it stands redeemed, employed as a constructive means to foster personal growth and improve interpersonal relationships. The Enneagram has thus evolved, shedding its mystical, esoteric cloak to wear the more pragmatic attire of psychological profiling.

So, as you step back and look at the winding path the Enneagram has journeyed, you find a narrative that is many things —mysterious, enriching, controversial, but never dull. Like a good historical document, it provides more questions than answers, urging us to continue exploring. The Enneagram, thus, is not just a mirror reflecting our individual identities; it's a window offering a glimpse into the collective wisdom and follies of human civilization across ages. And the view, I must say, is quite fascinating.

Modern Foundations and Cross-Cultural Synthesis

In the history of thought, some ideas become crucibles where various cultural elements fuse to create something new, something universally intriguing. The Enneagram is one such intriguing concept. Its development over the 20th century offers a narrative filled with intellectual voyages, arriving at a place where it stands today as a bridge between ancient wisdom and contemporary understanding.

Let's first turn our gaze towards George Ivanovich Gurdjieff, a name that even today resonates in discussions about the Enneagram. His role was not that of a path-breaking creator but more of a connector who brought disparate threads of Eastern and Western philosophies together. He saw the Enneagram as a sort of universal blueprint that could represent cosmic laws and human dynamics. This was not just mere academic dabbling; Gurdjieff had a mission to show that human understanding converges at some essential truths. The Enneagram, in his eyes, was a symbol powerful enough to illuminate these convergences.

Following this fascinating beginning came Oscar Ichazo from Bolivia. A man of profound learning, he channelled his wide-ranging studies into creating the Arica School. This school was not just an institution but a platform where Ichazo could share a lifetime's worth of wisdom. Importantly, it was through this conduit that the Enneagram made its way into the United States, finding resonance in the burgeoning New Age movements of the time. While the original teachings from Ichazo contained a comprehensive system of 108 Enneagrams, the U.S. adopted a more focused approach. Several key concepts gained traction, such as the Enneagram of the Passions and the Enneagram of the Virtues.

What sets Ichazo apart is his skill in linking the Enneagram with metaphysical aspects like Essence and personality. He opened doors to investigate the layers that shape human existence—from inherent traits to learned behaviours. His work also drew upon a variety of sources, from Plato's Divine Forms to the mystical Kabbalistic traditions. He effectively synthesized these ideas into a coherent Enneagram framework, shedding light on how one transitions from their true self to the personas shaped by societal norms and personal experiences. Another notable contributor is Claudio Naranjo, a Chilean psychologist who expanded the Enneagram's reach. Naranjo is notable for how he made the Enneagram accessible across cultural lines, underlining its intrinsic flexibility. The universal appeal of the Enneagram owes much to his ability to render its complex patterns relatable to a broad audience. It's not just a Western or Eastern concept; it is becoming a global one, reflecting the collective human experience.

So, what we see is a journey still in progress. From Gurdjieff's early adaptations to Ichazo's structural contributions and Naranjo's universal application, the Enneagram continues to evolve. It's like an ever-expanding discussion, where every insight adds a new layer, each thinker brings a new dimension, and every culture offers a fresh perspective. The Enneagram stands today as an amalgamation of wisdom from multiple times and places.

Like a historian peeling back the layers of an old manuscript, it allows us to delve into the complex tapestry of human behaviour and personality. This narrative, while rooted in individual contributions, is fundamentally a collective endeavour. It's similar to a large-scale, ongoing dialogue where the agenda is nothing short of understanding the nuanced labyrinth of human existence. It's a dialogue that still has room for new voices, for as we move through the 21st century, the Enneagram's role in exploring the depths of our collective psyche promises to be as relevant as ever.

What is Enneagram

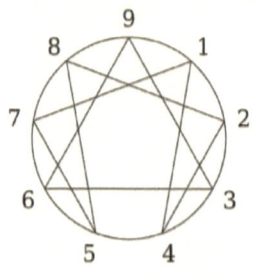

Having explored the historical contours of the Enneagram, let's now delve into its structural facets. The Enneagram model is less a static chart and more a dynamic ecosystem of human personality traits. Picture a circle with nine equidistant points; each point signifies a distinct personality type. These types bear specific names, such as "The Helper", "The Achiever", or "The Peacemaker", which are more than just labels. They encapsulate a set of characteristics, ways of thinking, and even potential pitfalls unique to each type. What brings depth to the Enneagram is not just the nine primary types, but also the lines that connect them. Think of these lines as roads in a sprawling city, facilitating movement and interaction between the neighborhoods of personality. When under stress or in a state of relaxation, an individual might find themselves taking one of these roads, exhibiting traits associated with another type. For instance, a steadfast "Loyalist" might show characteristics of an "Enthusiast" when in a more relaxed or optimistic mood.

But the Enneagram doesn't stop at mapping out these direct routes between types. In its complexity, it also includes "wings", which are the adjacent types that influence your core type. If you're predominantly an "Achiever", your behavior might still lean a bit towards either a "Helper" or an "Individualist", the numbers adjacent to "Achiever" on the Enneagram circle. These wings add another layer to the intricate human personality, showing that none of us are solely a product of our primary type. Moreover, the system is informed by various levels within each type, which range from healthy to average to unhealthy. This reflects the emotional and psychological state of an individual at a given time, demonstrating that while your core type remains the same, different circumstances can bring out varying aspects of your personality.

So, there you have it—the Enneagram in its elementary form, yet rich in depth and application. The system doesn't claim to solve the enigma of human personality; rather, it offers a structured pathway to navigate its intricacies. It's a tool that provides the language to discuss, analyze, and reflect upon the complexities of human behavior, for academics and laymen alike. The narrative of the Enneagram is a patchwork quilt, stitched together by a range of thinkers across different times and places. Its versatility is its strength, making it relevant across cultures and eras. And so, it has not merely remained a static concept but has evolved into an ever-expanding dialogue that accommodates a range of perspectives. Each contributor adds a layer to the concept's rich history, from its mystical beginnings to its current applications in diverse fields. The Enneagram has morphed from an esoteric symbol into a widely recognized and useful tool for understanding the complexities of human behaviour.

A Continuing Narrative

In the latter half of the 20th century, significant contributions came from people like Helen Palmer, Don Richard Riso, and Russ Hudson. These individuals have taken the Enneagram from the periphery of metaphysical studies into the mainstream of psychology and self-help.

Let's begin by acknowledging the pivotal roles played by Russ Hudson and Don Richard Riso. Together, they took the complex terrain of the Enneagram and made it navigable for everyday people. Their work can be considered the most detailed modern psychological account of the system. The "Riso-Hudson Enneagram Type Indicator" is, to this day, one of the most reliable tools to identify one's Enneagram type. They used the academic's rigor and the writer's skill to clarify and disseminate what was once arcane wisdom, repackaging it into practical advice for self-improvement.

Whereas Ichazo and Naranjo were rooted in blending diverse philosophical elements, Hudson and Riso took a more pragmatic approach. They placed the Enneagram squarely within the reach of the common individual, positioning it as a tool for personal development and emotional well-being. Their interpretation doesn't require a deep dive into esoteric philosophy or ancient wisdom; instead, it asks for introspection and self-reflection. In doing so, they ensured that the Enneagram would find its place not just in intellectual or spiritual circles but also in mainstream psychology.

Helen Palmer, another significant figure, approached the Enneagram with an emphasis on intuition and psychological states. She became one of the first authors to write texts that appealed to a Western audience, at times unfamiliar with philosophical or spiritual discourse. Her role was pivotal in making the Enneagram versatile, lending its principles to everything from personal growth to workplace dynamics. She stood as a bridge, connecting the abstract world of ideas with practical, everyday experiences. A distinct but equally important voice in this narrative is Beatrice Chestnut. Her focus was on the Enneagram's 'subtypes', taking us back to its complex layers. Chestnut's contributions have given a new depth to our understanding of each type, digging deeper into the nuances and variations that exist within the basic nine categories. While some were simplifying, she made it more intricate but understandable, keeping the intellectual rigor intact as the concept gained widespread popularity. Both Palmer and Chestnut, like Hudson and Riso before them, were translators of sorts. They took the academic and the esoteric and turned them into the accessible and the practical. In doing so, they democratized the Enneagram, making it a subject not just for the intellectual or the spiritual seeker but for the average person interested in understanding themselves better.

Today, the Enneagram's influence has expanded beyond just personal introspection. It's deployed in a variety of sectors like business, politics, and even crime studies. For instance, in organizational settings, the Enneagram lends insights into team dynamics and leadership styles. In politics, it has become a tool for understanding the motivations that drive leaders. In the realm of crime studies, it offers fresh perspectives on human behaviour and the underlying reasons for deviance. Even therapists now employ it as a framework to guide individuals through their emotional and psychological landscapes.

✳✳✳

Chapter Three

Learning Enneagram

So you've picked up this book, intrigued by the Enneagram or Numerology. Let's be clear, this is your starting point, your introduction to a world that's both ancient and endlessly fascinating. Think of it as standing on the shore of a vast ocean you're about to explore. We're not diving into the deep end just yet; we're merely dipping our toes in the water to feel its temperature.

The Enneagram and its nine personality types offer an incredible roadmap to understanding human behaviour. But here, we're only setting out on the first leg of the journey. Imagine you're in a grand library. We'll skim through the first pages of a few intriguing books, preparing you for the sagas that lie ahead. In the same way, this book is your starter kit. It's like your first-ever cricket match. You won't become Don Bradman or Brian Lara immediately, but you'll learn the basic rules, how to hold the bat, and maybe even hit a few shots. And just like cricket helps you understand teamwork and strategy, here you'll start to see hints of your own personality coming to light.

Becoming an expert in these mystical arts is a journey, not a two-minute Maggi noodles recipe. Consider this book the first few spices in your curry. It will add some flavour, but there's much more to the dish. You'll take part in workshops, read more books, and chat with people who think differently. It's like a laboratory where you perform little experiments to observe how numbers or personality types manifest in real life. Understanding the labyrinth of the human mind is no small task. But remember, this is a beginner's maze, simpler and smaller, designed to give you a taste of the challenge ahead. This book doesn't have all the answers; instead, it shows you how to start asking the right questions. It hands you the first few pieces of a grand puzzle, leaving you curious to find the rest.

So, in the vast ocean of the Enneagram or Numerology, consider this your first step into the water. We'll take you through the initial laps, enough to get you hooked but leaving plenty for you to explore and discover on your own. Every grand tapestry started with a single thread, and every expert was once a beginner. Now that we've set the stage, are you ready to take those first steps? Because the road ahead, my friend, is long but fascinating, and this is where it all begins. Shall we?

The Enneagram System

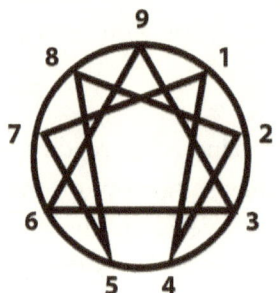

In the Enneagram framework, we come across nine specific personality types. Each of these types offers a unique lens through which people view and interact with the world. Think of these as foundational building blocks that help us get a clearer understanding of human behavior and motivations. cLet's check what are the nine types of Enneagram.

Type 1 - The Reformer : The Reformer is a perfectionist at heart. They are usually very disciplined and adhere to high moral standards. They like things to be fair and correct. If you notice someone who keeps talking about the "right way" of doing things, or who gets stressed when things are chaotic or inefficient, you're likely encountering a Type One. They are the ones who strive for improvement constantly. Practitioners will find it beneficial to focus on relaxing the perfectionistic tendencies of Type Ones.

Type 2 - The Helper : These individuals are all about relationships and helping others. They are often warm and nurturing. If someone is always there to lend a helping hand, puts others' needs before their own, and seems to feed off social interactions, it is quite possible that you are dealing with a Type Two. This type benefits from learning to establish boundaries and taking time for self-care.

Type 3 - The Achiever : Highly success-driven, Type Threes are the overachievers in any group. They are goal-oriented and don't like wasting time. They tend to be competitive, focusing on status and image. Spotting a Type Three is relatively easy: look for ambition, a focus on achievement, and a potential for workaholism. Practitioners should help Threes slow down and appreciate their intrinsic worth beyond accomplishments.

Type 4 - The Individualist : People falling under this category are usually emotionally intense and have a flair for drama. They believe they are unique and different. If someone keeps talking about their distinct perspectives or emotions, tends to get lost in daydreams, and loves exploring their inner world, you've likely got a Type Four. Practitioners should aim to ground these types in the reality of common human experiences, thereby mitigating feelings of being perpetually 'different'.

Type 5 - The Investigator : Curiosity marks this type. Type Fives prefer observing from a distance and are usually introverted. They love to collect information and often have expertise in unexpected areas. A person who seems more interested in ideas or books than in social interactions can often be categorized as a Type Five. For this type, practitioners should focus on encouraging more active engagement with the world.

Type 6 - The Loyalist : If someone is always prepared, questions everything, and tends to worry a lot, they are likely a Type Six. They often seek guidance or rules to make sense of the world. Practitioners will find that Type Six individuals benefit from learning to trust themselves and gaining confidence in their decision-making abilities.

Type 7 - The Enthusiast : This is the type that loves to explore new opportunities. They are spontaneous and don't like to be restricted by schedules or rules. If you notice someone who is always excited about the next big thing and hates being bored, you've likely encountered a Type Seven. Practitioners should help Sevens to focus and appreciate the present moment, rather than always looking to the next big thing.

Type 8 - The Challenger : Powerful and dominating, Type Eights take charge of situations. They are proactive and know how to get things done. They often have a protective streak. If you see someone who isn't afraid to express their opinions boldly and takes the initiative, you are likely dealing with a Type Eight. Practitioners can guide Eights in understanding the power of vulnerability.

Type 9 - The Peacemaker : Lastly, Type Nines are easy-going and hate conflicts. They prefer to keep the peace and are generally quite accommodating and open-minded. If you know someone who is always avoiding conflicts and seems to go along with what everyone else wants, they might be a Type Nine. Practitioners should help Nines to realize that their opinions and desires are important too.

When we study each personality type in detail, we unearth the core traits that define it. This process helps in two significant ways. First, it enables us to discover more about ourselves. We become aware of why we act in certain ways and what drives our actions. Second, it improves our interactions with others. When we understand the basics of someone's personality, we can communicate and collaborate more effectively. This is not just theoretical knowledge; it has practical implications in daily life. It becomes a useful guide for self-improvement and helps us better manage our relationships, be it at home, work, or in social settings.

Remember, each person is unique, and while these categories provide a useful framework, they are just that—frameworks. However, a seasoned practitioner can use this guide as a starting point to delve deeper into understanding their clients' or subjects' psychological and emotional landscapes. Understanding the core motivations and fears can provide profound insights into the driving forces behind each Enneagram type's behaviours and actions. It's important to remember that each type possesses both strengths and limitations, and the Enneagram journey is about embracing the full spectrum of human nature.

Let's look into the core motivations and fears of each type in the next page.

Type	Core Motivation	Core Fear
Type 1	Striving for integrity and improvement. Ones are driven by a need to do what is right, just, and moral.	Fear of being corrupt, defective, or morally wrong. Ones dread making mistakes or failing to meet their own high standards.
Type 2	Seeking love and appreciation. Twos are motivated by a desire to be needed, valued, and loved by assisting and supporting others.	Fear of being unloved, unwanted, or rejected. Twos worry that if they don't meet others' needs, they will lose their connections.
Type 3	Striving for success and recognition. Threes are driven to achieve goals, gain recognition, and present a positive image to the world.	Fear of being worthless or a failure. Threes worry that without success or admiration, they are insignificant.
Type 4	Seeking identity and significance. Fours are motivated to find their unique identity and experience deep, authentic emotions.	Fear of being mundane or ordinary. Fours worry that they lack a sense of identity and will be overlooked.
Type 5	Pursuing knowledge and understanding. Fives are driven to gather information and insights, seeking to understand the world around them.	Fear of being overwhelmed or invaded. Fives dread feeling incapable of handling their surroundings or being emotionally overwhelmed.
Type 6	Seeking security and support. Sixes are motivated by a need for safety, loyalty, and guidance in an uncertain world.	Fear of being unsupported or without guidance. Sixes worry about being abandoned or facing threats without help.
Type 7	Pursuing joy and variety. Sevens are driven to experience pleasure, excitement, and to avoid pain by seeking new opportunities.	Fear of being trapped or limited. Sevens dread feeling trapped in negative emotions or mundane routines.
Type 8	Seeking control and strength. Eights are motivated to be in control, protect the vulnerable, and demonstrate their strength.	Fear of being controlled or vulnerable. Eights worry about being manipulated or taken advantage of by others.
Type 9	Seeking inner peace and harmony. Nines are motivated by a desire to maintain a calm and conflict-free environment.	Fear of conflict or separation. Conflict and tension, fearing that it will disrupt their inner peace and connection with others.

Chapter Four

The Enneagram Symbol

A simple yet complexly powerful geometry

Imagine gazing at the Enneagram symbol, a seemingly simple yet profoundly meaningful design. Within its intricate patterns lies a wealth of wisdom that transcends time and culture. This symbol not only encapsulates the essence of our existence but also acts as a portal to the ancient knowledge systems that have shaped human understanding for millennia. As we explore the significance of the Enneagram symbol, we uncover its deep roots in complex geometries and diverse spiritual traditions, highlighting its role as a bridge between the past and the present.

The Enneagram symbol has been a subject of keen interest across various disciplines and cultures. It's simple geometric shape—a circle with a triangle and hexad inside—has been a canvas for intricate interpretations. The term "Enneagram" is derived from Greek, where 'Ennea' means nine and 'gram' refers to a drawing or figure. Though the geometric form is straightforward, the origins of this intriguing symbol are quite complex and multifaceted.

Starting with the Pythagorean connection, there is speculation that Pythagoras, the ancient Greek mathematician and philosopher, developed the Enneagram symbol during his time in Heliopolis. Heliopolis was an ancient Egyptian city known for its scholars and libraries. Pythagoras, who believed

Decoding You

that geometry was a way to understand the divine, might have conceptualized the Enneagram as a representation of universal laws and harmonies.

Another theory points to Christian mysticism. Early Christian priests and scholars have been thought to employ symbols similar to the Enneagram in their theological studies. Though not exactly the Enneagram as we know it, these symbols were used as tools for contemplation and understanding the divine nature. Such a correlation suggests that the Enneagram symbol might have Christian roots or at least parallel developments within Christian mysticism. The Jewish Kabbalah also provides a compelling angle. Kabbalistic scholars emphasize the sacredness of numbers and geometric figures. In this tradition, the Tree of Life—a symbol with ten interconnected nodes—shares similarities with the Enneagram. Both symbols aim to represent the complexities of life and the divine, making them kindred spirits in the world of ancient symbols. When it comes to similarities with other symbols, the Enneagram bears a close resemblance to other geometric constructs used across ancient cultures. For example, the Sri Yantra in Hinduism, an intricate design of nine interlocking triangles, shares the nine-pointed structure. The Borromean Rings, another mathematical figure with three interlocking circles, also echo the theme of interconnectedness found in the Enneagram.

George Gurdjieff, a 20th-century spiritual teacher, reintroduced the Enneagram symbol, but his focus was more on its cosmological implications. His interpretations were not aligned with any specific religious or philosophical tradition but rather aimed to encapsulate universal principles and laws governing the cosmos. Bolivian psychologist Oscar Ichazo was instrumental in giving the Enneagram symbol its modern psychological twist, associating its nine points with specific human personality traits. However, this paper concentrates on the Enneagram as a symbol, devoid of its psychological interpretations.

The Enneagram symbol's complexity and adaptability have made it a subject of interest across various fields including spirituality, psychology, and business strategy. Over time, the symbol has absorbed elements from different intellectual traditions, making it a multidimensional entity of study.

***

The Enneagram and Pentagram

The pentagram, a five-pointed star enclosed in a circle, has a long and varied history across different cultures. Originally seen in Mesopotamian writings around 3500 BCE, the symbol has taken on various roles and meanings over time. In ancient Greece, the pentagram was known as the "Pentalpha", comprised of five interlocking A-shaped alphabets. It was a symbol associated with the goddess Hygeia, who represents health. In medieval times, The Christian Church adopted the pentagram as a protective emblem.

The Enneagram and the Pentagram

Christian traditions interpreted the five points as the five wounds of Christ. But with the passage of time, its interpretation evolved—or rather, devolved—into being associated with the occult and witchcraft, especially during the late medieval period. Fast forward to the 20th century, the pentagram has become an emblem in modern spirituality, especially Wiccan and Neopagan traditions. Here it is seen as a representation of the five elements: earth, water, air, fire, and spirit, each represented by a point of the star. On the scientific side, the pentagram is often highlighted for its geometric perfection. It incorporates the Golden Ratio, a mathematical proportion found in many natural phenomena, making it a subject of interest not just for spiritual leaders but also for mathematicians and scientists.

The Enneagram, meanwhile, is a symbol that features nine points and is best known for its application in personality typing. Its roots are harder to trace but are often attributed to spiritual traditions like Sufism and early forms of Christianity. The nine points are seen as a guide to human nature and psychological tendencies, offering a structured approach to self-understanding and personal growth.

Despite their different origins and primary uses, the pentagram and the Enneagram share key thematic similarities. Both are concerned with the human journey towards balance and completeness. The pentagram, through its representation of elemental balance, emphasizes the unity of elements and spiritual equilibrium, advocates for harmony in our relationship with the natural world. The Enneagram, on the other hand, suggests that understanding and integrating different facets of our personality can lead to a more balanced and fulfilling life. The spiritual and scientific convergence of the Enneagram and the pentagram highlights their shared goal of uncovering the hidden layers of existence. Both symbols encourage self-awareness, transformation, and an exploration of the intricate threads that weave together our individual experiences and the greater cosmos.

On a broader level, both symbols hint at a universal order. Whether it is the mathematical precision of the Golden Ratio in the pentagram or the structured typology of human nature in the Enneagram, the message is clear: our complex world and intricate personalities are not random or chaotic but guided by underlying principles that we can understand and apply in our lives. The pentagram and the Enneagram, while rooted in different traditions and applied in different contexts, serve as complementary tools for exploring the complexities of existence, be it our relationship with the external world or our internal psychological landscapes. They offer a structured approach to understanding the different dimensions of human experience, drawing on both spiritual beliefs and scientific principles.

※※※

Contrast with other cultures

The Enneagram has piqued human curiosity with its detailed geometric structure and insightful take on the human psyche. It's intriguing to note that this relatively modern concept shares similarities with ancient symbols like Padmas and Yantras, stemming from spiritual traditions such as Tantric, Buddhist, and Vedic philosophies.

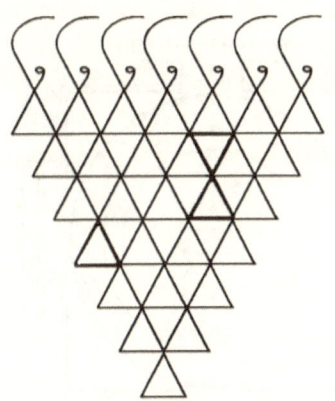

The Saraswati Yantra

In these ancient spiritual pathways, the Padma, or the lotus flower, holds a significant place. The lotus is a symbol of purity and spiritual enlightenment, illustrating a journey from the dimness of ignorance to the light of wisdom. The Enneagram serves a similar purpose, offering a route for self-discovery and personal growth. Designed as a circle with nine points, each point symbolizes a distinct personality type. Both the Padma and the Enneagram stress that real growth arises from acknowledging the hidden complexities within us, not unlike the way a lotus flower rises through muddy waters to bloom under the sun.

Transitioning to Yantras, these are intricate geometric designs rooted in Tantric and Vedic traditions. Intended as objects of meditation, Yantras serve to establish a link between human consciousness and higher spiritual dimensions. They are viewed as encapsulations of cosmic energies and archetypal principles. Similarly, the Enneagram operates as a geometric outline of the human psyche. It grants keen insights into how the mind and emotions function. While Yantras serve as portals to divine wisdom, the Enneagram functions as a gateway to a greater self-awareness and individual progression.

Among Yantras, the Sri Yantra stands out for its geometric sophistication. It combines triangles, circles, and floral patterns to create a balanced visual composition. This particular Yantra symbolizes the union of masculine and feminine divine energies. At its core, nine interlocking triangles offer a holistic perspective of the universe and the principles behind creation. The central point, known as the "bindu", signifies the starting point of existence. Therefore, the Sri Yantra provides a concentrated focus for meditation, leading practitioners towards enlightened states of mind.

In Buddhism, Mandalas serve as another example of sacred geometry akin to the Enneagram. Mainly utilized in meditation, Mandalas aim to guide individuals from a state of ignorance to enlightenment. Both Mandalas and the Enneagram underscore the cyclical nature of human life, implying that fluctuations are an inherent part of the transformative journey.

The Sri Yantra

The commonalities between the Enneagram, Padmas, and Yantras suggest the presence of universal principles across different spiritual frameworks. These symbols go beyond mere artistic designs; they act as sophisticated tools for fostering deeper self-understanding and spiritual growth. This connection solidifies the notion that the pursuit of spiritual enlightenment and self-awareness is a shared human experience. It's worth recognizing that the Enneagram's resemblance to symbols like Padmas and Yantras signifies a certain unity in spiritual explorations across diverse cultural landscapes. Identifying these common patterns can reveal enduring truths that have influenced human endeavours for centuries. The convergence of these symbols from different traditions suggests a multifaceted human experience, unified by mutual quests for self-discovery, spiritual development, and a fundamental curiosity about our place in the universe. Indeed, adding the dimension of Kabbalah Numerology, particularly its Tree of Life, deepens our conversation about these spiritual symbols. Just like the Enneagram, the Tree of Life is not just a simple figure; it's a detailed map filled with spiritual insights. It connects what we think of as divine with our everyday life, drawing parallels with the Enneagram's quest for self-awareness.

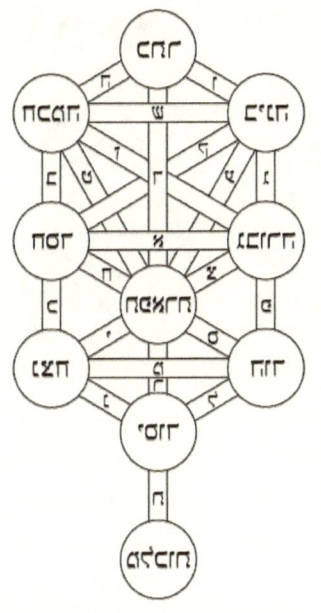

The Tree of Life

Both of these tools—be it the nine-pointed Enneagram or the complex Tree of Life—offer us navigational aids in the sometimes-confusing journey of human emotions and motivations. The Enneagram's nine facets explore different types of personalities and the hidden abilities within them. On the other hand, the Kabbalah Tree of Life shows us how various divine qualities appear in our own human experiences.

When we look at different symbols like the Enneagram, Padmas, Yantras, Buddhist Mandalas, and the Kabbalah 'Tree of Life', we see they are all part of a bigger picture. These symbols go beyond the barriers of language, culture, and history. Although each symbol comes from a different spiritual background, they all aim to help us understand ourselves and how we fit into the universe.

To sum up, the Enneagram, along with Padmas, Yantras, Mandalas, and the Kabbalah Tree of Life, act as reflective surfaces. They mirror not just our individual goals for spiritual growth and self-awareness but also our collective human endeavour for a deeper understanding of life. These symbols, rooted in varied spiritual traditions, underline the universal nature of certain quests that remain constant throughout human history. These quests, whether for spiritual development, self-awareness, or understanding our relationship with the cosmos, are markers on the roadmap of human existence, directing us toward our boundless potential for growth and understanding.

✳✳✳

Anatomy of Enneagram Symbol

The Enneagram symbol brings together three shapes: a circle, a triangle, and a hexad. Each shape has its own meaning, rooted in universal laws.

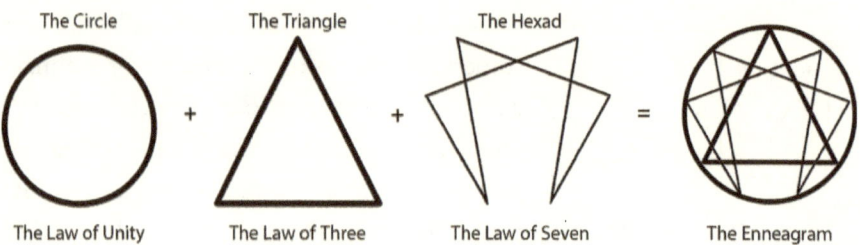

Let's start with the circle. It represents the Law of Unity. In simpler terms, the circle tells us that everything is connected. This isn't just about being one with the world; it also applies to smaller aspects like personal growth and social dynamics. In essence, unity triumphs over division. Next comes the triangle within the circle, standing for the Law of Three. This law helps us understand how change happens. Think of it like a project: you have planning (active), execution (passive), and then feedback (reconciling). All these three elements must work in harmony for any meaningful transformation. The third shape, the hexad, symbolizes the Law of Seven. This shape teaches us that life is not a straight line. Progress occurs in cycles, and it's rarely without ups and downs. The Law of Seven urges us to look at life as a journey full of different phases rather than a single, straightforward path.

When you bring all these shapes together, you get the Enneagram symbol. It serves as a comprehensive model for understanding not just human behaviour but also the laws that govern the universe. It's not just a diagram but a holistic system that can guide us through life's complexities.

Now, let's talk about how these shapes relate to each other. The journey from the hexad and triangle towards the circle can be seen as moving from chaos to unity. At the start, you're dealing with complexities—whether in personal relationships, work, or inner conflicts. It might feel overwhelming. But as you move metaphorically towards the circle, complexities begin to appear simpler. The overarching Law of Unity comes into focus. Why does this matter? Because it's not just a map for personal growth but also a guide for how we fit into the larger universe. The Law of Unity tells us that despite the chaos and complexities we encounter, there's a greater unity that binds us all. This concept is rooted in various philosophies across the world, including Indian traditions that talk about the oneness of individual and universal soul.

The Law of Unity

The Enneagram—a geometric shape that encompasses much more than mere lines and angles—serves as a guide to human psychology and spirituality. At its core lies a circle. A circle that symbolizes Unity. When we talk about unity in the context of the Enneagram, it isn't merely a harmonious blend of different elements but an interdependent existence that moves beyond our understanding of diversity and individuality. Think of it as the foundational fabric of life. A fabric that is not visible to the naked eye but permeates every interaction, every thought, and every emotion.

Before we tread further on this path, let's question the basic premise: What is unity? Is it mere coherence or homogeneity? In a world populated by myriad species, shaped by countless cultures, and influenced by various philosophies, it seems rather contradictory to speak of unity. Yet, it's this paradox that the Law of Unity under the Enneagram attempts to resolve. It does not negate diversity but subsumes it, like a river that accommodates various streams without losing its essence. This concept of Unity extends to not just interpersonal relationships but to our intrinsic connection with the universe.

Here's a proposition. Let us take it not as an axiom but as a perspective, open to scrutiny. The human experience is a collective phenomenon. Whether we acknowledge it or not, our thoughts, actions, and feelings aren't isolated occurrences. They are intertwined, much like threads in a cloth, with the threads being not just the people but every element of this world. This connectedness is what the circle in the Enneagram represents. It doesn't have a beginning or an end; it's an uninterrupted continuum that encapsulates the sum total of human experiences and transcends them. In the psychological realm, the implications are significant. Our thoughts aren't just a string of neural reactions but are tied to our emotions and actions. They exist not in a vacuum but in a milieu of past experiences, cultural conditioning, and future aspirations. Here, the Law of Unity impels us to think beyond the 'self', to see our emotions and actions not just as isolated occurrences but as interconnected elements in the broader canvas of human interaction. This is more than mere intellectual understanding; it is an experiential truth, one that fosters empathy and enriches our social lives.

Let's also glance through a spiritual lens. In a society driven by labels—nationalities, religions, and ideologies—the concept of unity appears elusive, even utopian. But the Enneagram tells us otherwise. It tells us that our connections run deep, beyond these surface identifiers. When we internalize this Law of Unity, our perception shifts. The focus then is not on the 'other' but on a common essence that is far more integral than these divisions. Spirituality here is not about detachment but about profound attachment to a grander scheme, where every entity has value, and all energies converge towards unity. To fully grasp this is akin to the realization that we are mere droplets in an infinite ocean, separate yet intrinsically part of a larger whole. The Enneagram takes it a notch further by emphasizing that each individual embodies elements of all nine types. A reminder that we are both unique and universal. Imagine a puzzle, every piece unique but incomplete on its own. The beauty unfolds when they come together, each adding value to the other, and what emerges is a mosaic that is as diverse as it is unified.

This isn't a notion to be romanticized but to be lived. As we navigate through the corridors of Enneagram wisdom, the challenge is to extend these understandings from the self to the society and to the universe. It's about seeing the world not as fragments but as a unified whole, where even the distinctions add value, creating a dynamic, ever-evolving tapestry. It's a transformative journey, one that requires us to first accept and then to transcend our individual limitations to connect with the infinite. The Enneagram and its Law of Unity do not offer a panacea for all the world's complexities, but they provide a lens to better comprehend them. It's not about crafting an alternate reality but about understanding the existing one, in all its diversity and contradictions. And perhaps, in that understanding lies the key to a life richer in empathy, purpose, and above all, unity.

The Law of Three

The Law of Three in the Enneagram is like a crucial guidebook. It's akin to a manual that's aimed not just at understanding ourselves better but also at grasping the complexity of the world around us. This law is represented by a triangle that links the points 9, 3, and 6. And at its very core, this law focuses on explaining the human personality through three main forces: the Active, the Passive, and the Neutralizing. Now, you might wonder why these forces are so important. They are significant because they act like characters in our life's story. Some take the lead, shaping the events. Some take a step back, offering support. And some bring balance when things seem to go off track. The beauty lies in the interplay of these forces. Understanding which force is dominant in our lives helps us figure out our tendencies, habits, and even the recurring themes in our experiences.

Let's dig a bit deeper into the psychology of it. When you identify which force is taking charge in your life, a lot of puzzles get solved. Why do we react the way we do? Why do some situations trigger us more than others? These are not just random events but a result of the dominant force in our personality. If the Active force is more prominent, you might find yourself taking charge often. If it's the Passive force, maybe you are more of a supporter in situations. And if it's the Neutralizing force, you're probably the one who brings balance when there's conflict.

But the Law of Three isn't just about introspection; it's also about understanding the wider world. It's like a map that doesn't only show your neighbourhood but shows how it connects to the whole city. Within the framework of the Enneagram, different personality types are not isolated islands but parts of a larger continent. They share mutual influences; they are interdependent. In simple terms, we all are linked. Our actions and thoughts don't just impact us but have a ripple effect on others as well.

This ripple effect is most visible when we talk about spirituality or religion. Many religious traditions have the concept of the Trinity: Father, Son, and Holy Spirit. The Law of Three fits well into this spiritual outlook. It tells us that just as God has multiple dimensions, so does reality. This understanding is a game-changer. It nudges us to see divinity not as a single entity up in the sky but as an omnipresent force, with multiple facets that are found even in day-to-day life. Lastly, how does this law affect our perspective on change? Life is never a straight line; it's more like a roller coaster with its peaks and valleys. And this law offers a blueprint for navigating through this roller coaster. It tells us that change happens through cycles—there's a time for action, a time for stepping back, and a time for bringing things into balance. Understanding this gives us the mental tools to deal with life's challenges. It doesn't promise a life without problems, but it certainly equips us to handle them better.

The Law of Seven

When you first lay eyes on the Hexad, it may seem like just another six-pointed geometric shape. But give it time, and you'll notice the incredible depth hidden within its lines. This six-pointed figure is a representation of the Law of Seven, a concept that explores the cyclical and non-linear paths we follow in life. Though it consists of six points, it is the seventh point—the one where the cycle loops back to its origin—that gives it meaning. In a way, the Hexad encapsulates life's complexities, helping us visualize a journey filled with stops and starts, highs and lows.

The Hexad is not just a random figure; it's a blueprint. Let's understand its relation to the Law of Seven. Imagine you are on a quest to reach a destination. Your journey doesn't take you straight from point A to B; it's more like a zigzag path. This is where the Hexad comes in handy. Each of the six points on the Hexad symbolizes a change in momentum—a bump on the road, if you will. Maybe it's the rush of excitement you feel when you first embark on a new endeavour. Maybe it's the obstacle you didn't foresee, making you question your journey. Perhaps it's a moment of enlightenment, where you finally see the bigger picture, urging you to push forward. Each point offers a pause for reflection and adjustment.

Let's delve into this a bit more. The Law of Seven explains that our path is never a straight line but a series of rising and falling energies. This might sound abstract, so let's make it more relatable. Consider the process of learning to ride a bicycle. Initially, the energy is high—full of excitement and enthusiasm. Then you experience the first fall, and your energy dips. You ponder whether to continue. That's your first change in momentum. After some struggle, you find balance, and the energy rises again, propelling you forward. Another point on the Hexad. The cycle continues, each point a marker of your journey—until you reach the seventh point, the origin, where you find mastery. It's as though the seven points—six external and one at the core—map out not just the physical journey but also the emotional and intellectual arcs.

Philosophers have contemplated the Law of Seven for ages, seeing it as a universal concept that governs everything from human behaviour to the cosmos. George Gurdjieff, a significant figure in this area, provided the idea with a layer of spiritual nuance. According to him, the path of life is a sequence of octaves, and the Hexad offers a geometric representation of this sequence. Gurdjieff believed that understanding the Hexad and the Law of Seven could guide us in various aspects of life, be it spiritual growth or mundane activities.

And while this Law of Seven has ancient roots, its application is not confined to scholarly discussions. Take the realm of management, for instance. Many leadership models highlight the importance of agility and adaptability. The Hexad, and by extension, the Law of Seven, provides a framework to navigate the complex landscape of decision-making. Each point on the Hexad can be a stage of evaluating, strategizing, and recalibrating. In doing so, the Hexad becomes more than just a theoretical construct; it becomes a tool for practical wisdom.

To wrap it up, the Hexad is not merely a six-pointed figure; it's a life guide compressed into geometry. It teaches us that journeys are seldom straightforward; they are rather a series of ups and downs, each an opportunity for learning and growth. And when you complete the cycle, hitting the seventh point, it's not an end but a new beginning, urging you to embark on another journey, but with a newer more enlightened perspective.

✳✳✳

The Bigger Picture

Life is often a series of pixels, tiny fragments that occupy our immediate attention. Each pixel may represent a problem to solve, a person to meet, or a task to complete. So absorbed are we in these pixels that we forget they are but elements of a much larger image. The enneagram's internal hexad, a circle containing six points, mirrors this focus on the individual pixels, the micro aspects of daily living that claim our attention and resources.

Yet, what happens when we step back? When we zoom out from the immediate pixels and look at the screen as a whole? A different kind of understanding takes place. The chaos of colours and lines form an image, a picture that holds meaning, pattern, and even beauty. This is akin to the 'law of unity' in the enneagram—a reminder that life's beauty and meaning are often found not in individual moments but in the tapestry, they form when woven together.

By shifting our gaze from the pixels to the image, from the hexad to the law of unity, a transformation occurs within us. It's a transition from a state of scattered fragmentation to a state of wholeness. One begins to realize that the individual events, which once seemed so urgent and important, are part of a greater scheme. Our frustrations, anxieties, and daily struggles don't vanish but they find their rightful place in a broader context. This awareness brings a different quality of happiness. It's not the fleeting joy that comes from solving a problem or achieving a goal. It's a more enduring form of happiness that's rooted in a profound sense of connection with the larger world. It is not contingent upon external circumstances but arises from an inner alignment with life's deeper rhythms.

To grasp the law of unity is to move from fragmentation to wholeness, from chaos to harmony. Just as the pixels make sense only when seen as part of a whole image, so do the events of our life gain meaning when viewed in the context of a larger, unifying principle. In aligning ourselves with this principle, we do not escape our daily challenges but we face them with a different kind of intelligence, an intelligence not of separation but of connection, not of division but of unity.

While the enneagram philosophy originates from a different culture and context, the transition it describes—from the intricate web of daily concerns in the hexad to the more expansive 'law of unity'—finds a remarkable echo in Indian philosophy, particularly in Vedanta. In Vedanta, the concept of 'Moksha' captures a similar transition. Moksha is not just liberation from the cycle of birth and death; it's the realization of one's unity with the ultimate reality, often described as Brahman in Vedantic terms. When we are entangled in the myriad concerns of life—our jobs, relationships, ambitions—we are much like someone lost in the hexad, each point representing a different dimension of worldly existence. But Moksha encourages us to zoom out, to broaden our perspective and recognize that these are just pixels in a far grander image.

Once this state of awareness is reached, it leads to 'Chidanandam', a term often used in Vedantic literature to describe the bliss that emanates from the consciousness of unity with the universe. This isn't a transient joy that comes and goes with good or bad experiences; it's a deep-seated happiness, much like the enduring form of happiness one finds when aligning with the enneagram's law of unity. This happiness stems from a profound connection to the larger cosmos, an understanding that life's complexities and struggles are but tiny dots in a much larger canvas. This is akin to realizing that the chaos of individual pixels contributes to creating a beautiful, coherent image when viewed from a distance.

So, both the enneagram and Vedanta guide us toward the same truth: that life's challenges and struggles are not to be escaped but understood in a more expansive framework. They both suggest that our myopic concerns can be transcended, not by negating them, but by viewing them as part of something larger, something infinitely more significant. In this realization, we find a form of happiness and peace that is not dependent on external circumstances but is a natural outcome of our inner alignment with universal principles. Thus, while the enneagram may use different terms and symbols, its underlying message shares an uncanny resemblance with the Vedantic concepts of Moksha and Chidanandam. Both offer a lens through which to view life, encouraging us to move from a fractured understanding filled with immediate concerns to a more holistic perspective where individual worries dissolve into a larger, harmonious reality. This shift in perspective, whether achieved through the teachings of Vedanta or the symbolism of the enneagram, promises a kind of happiness that is both profound and enduring.

Therefore, the enneagram does not offer an escape from the world but a different way of being in it. It does not negate the individual struggles represented by the internal hexad but places them in the context of the law of unity. And in doing so, it invites us to a way of living where the pixels and the picture are in harmony, where the many and the one coexist, and where the understanding of this coexistence leads not to conflict but to a deep, abiding sense of peace.

❋❋❋

Chapter Five

Inner symphony of Enneagram

The captivating Centres of Intelligence and Wings

Enneagram typology, while primarily focused on unveiling the intricacies of individual personalities, also offers insights into the dynamics of relationships and compatibility between different types. This aspect of the Enneagram taps into the rich scenery of human interactions, shedding light on how different personalities can harmonize, clash, and evolve together. Understanding compatibility in the context of the Enneagram involves recognizing how various personality types interact, influence, and respond to each other. While each type possesses distinct qualities and tendencies, these traits can either complement or challenge those of another type. This dynamic interplay is a key feature of the Enneagram's holistic perspective on human relationships.

One way the Enneagram addresses compatibility is through the concept of wings. Each Enneagram type is believed to have adjacent types called wings. These wing types influence a person's core type, adding depth and nuance to their personality. For example, a Type 1 may have a Type 2 or Type 9 wing. Understanding the wings of one's own type can provide insights into potential areas of compatibility with neighbouring types.

Moreover, the Enneagram's lines of connection depict how different types can move toward the positive traits of another type when they are

Decoding You

experiencing growth, and conversely, how they can exhibit negative traits when under stress. This understanding opens a window into how relationships can impact personal growth and transformation. For instance, a Type 5, known for their analytical nature, may exhibit qualities of a healthier Type 8 (The Challenger) when growing, embracing assertiveness and action.

Centres of Intelligence

In the Enneagram system, the centres of intelligence are one way of categorizing and understanding how different personality types process information, emotions, and experiences. These centres are known as the Body Centre, the Heart Centre, and the Head Centre. Each centre corresponds to a specific way of perceiving and responding to the world, and individuals within the same centre often share certain patterns of behaviour, emotional reactions, and thought processes.

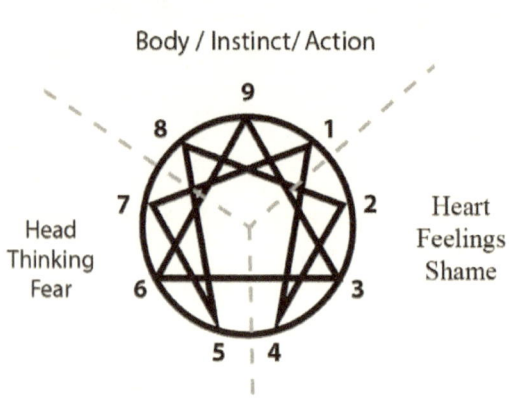

The compatibility of different types also relates to their centre of intelligence – the Body Centre, the Heart Centre, and the Head Centre. Types within the same centre often share common emotional and cognitive responses, which can either lead to harmony or conflict. Exploring how these centres interact within relationships provides valuable insights into communication patterns and potential areas of synergy.

1. Body Centre (Instinctive Centre) - The Body Centre encompasses types Eight, Nine, and One. Individuals within this centre tend to be more in touch with their physical sensations and instincts. They rely on their gut feelings and bodily cues to navigate the world. They often react instinctively to situations and prioritize action. This centre is associated with issues of control, anger, and instinctual responses.

- *Type Eight*: Focus on control, power, and autonomy. Can be assertive and protective but may struggle with vulnerability.
- *Type Nine*: Emphasis on peace, harmony, and maintaining stability. Tendency to avoid conflict and suppress their own needs.
- *Type One*: Driven by a desire for perfection, correctness, and improvement. May struggle with a critical inner voice.

2. **Heart Centre (Feeling Centre) -** The Heart Centre includes types Two, Three, and Four. People in this centre are more attuned to their emotions and often rely on their feelings to make decisions and understand their experiences. They value relationships and their self-worth is often tied to how they are perceived by others.

- *Type Two*: Driven by a need to be helpful, loved, and valued. Can be generous but might struggle with boundaries.
- *Type Three*: Strives for success, recognition, and efficiency. May have difficulty connecting with authentic feelings due to a focus on image.
- *Type Four*: Focus on individuality, emotions, and uniqueness. May experience intense emotions and struggle with feelings of inadequacy.

3. **Head Centre (Thinking Centre) -** The Head Centre encompasses types Five, Six, and Seven. Individuals in this centre rely heavily on their thoughts, analysis, and intellectual understanding of the world. They often grapple with anxiety and uncertainty.

- *Type Five*: Driven by a need for knowledge, understanding, and privacy. Can be withdrawn and may struggle with social interactions.
- *Type Six*: Concerned with security, loyalty, and planning. Tends to oscillate between seeking guidance and doubting oneself.
- *Type Seven*: Focus on variety, spontaneity, and avoiding pain. Might struggle with commitment and facing negative emotions.

Understanding these centres of intelligence can provide insights into why certain types behave the way they do, how they process information, and how they relate to others. It's important to note that while types within the same centre share common traits, each individual is unique and influenced by various factors beyond their Enneagram type. Exploring these centres can help improve communication, resolve conflicts, and foster better relationships by recognizing and appreciating different ways of perceiving and responding to the world. An important aspect of Enneagram compatibility is the recognition that every type has strengths and challenges. Partnerships between types can flourish when individuals recognize and appreciate each other's unique qualities. For instance, the analytical nature of a Type 5 can complement the enthusiasm of a Type 7, fostering a balanced and insightful relationship.

Understanding Wings

The Enneagram, often thought of as a straightforward diagram boxing us into one of nine personality categories, has more to offer than first meets the eye. It presents a deeper layer, frequently overlooked but essential—wings. Imagine these wings as the ingredients that elevate a simple daal to an aromatic daal makhani. The wings sit beside your main Enneagram type, bringing in complexities and nuances that make each personality uniquely fascinating, just as every individual in our diverse nation is.

A common belief suggests that a person is mainly defined by their core Enneagram type. While convenient, this overlooks the complexity that each human brings to the table. Consider a Type Nine individual, commonly known as the Peacemaker. Now, adjacent to this Type Nine are two wings—Eight and One. These wings add layers to the Peacemaker's core traits. It's as if the basic nature of the Type Nine is a plain canvas, and the wings—either Eight or One—provide the brushstrokes that make it a masterpiece. Pioneers like Don Richard Riso and Russ Hudson have thrown light on the significance of wings in the Enneagram. Riso views these wings as elements that enrich your core identity, akin to how varying hues add depth to a painting. Hudson draws a similar analogy, comparing wings to shades of colour that make the complete picture more vibrant. Just as a rainbow is incomplete without the harmony of its colours, an individual's Enneagram type lacks fullness without considering the wings.

An interesting aspect of wings is the debate on their number. While it's clear that each type has two adjacent wings, they don't usually influence the core type equally. Most people are swayed more by one wing than the other. For example, if you are a Type Two, commonly known as the Helper, you could lean towards either a Three-wing, known as the Achiever, or a One-wing, known as the Reformer. The lesser wing isn't absent; it just doesn't assert itself as strongly as the dominant one. Some experts also note that as people age or grow psychologically, the less dominant wing starts to become more influential. Whether this happens universally is a subject that beckons further study. Identifying your core Enneagram type is just the starting point. Tools like the Riso-Hudson Enneagram Type Indicator exist to help you pinpoint not just your core type but your potential wings. It's crucial to remember that these tools have limitations; they cannot encapsulate the intricacy of human personality. Real insight comes from reading extensively about your core type and observing how your wings manifest in different life situations.

Why bother with wings at all? Understanding your wing can offer pathways to personal growth. This knowledge can help you identify your motivations and fears. It also has broader implications for interpersonal relationships. Knowing your wings can illuminate why you connect easily with some people and find it difficult with others. Enneagram is not just a static circle but a dynamic model. Wings add a layer of richness to the primary types. They help us understand that we are more than just a singular number; we are a blend of different elements that together form our complex personalities. Just like the layers of history in an ancient city, these layers make us compelling, intricate, and profoundly human.

✳✳✳

The Dominant Wing: A Powerful Influence

Understanding your dominant wing in the Enneagram is somewhat like recognizing the dominant hand you use for writing. While both hands are a part of you, one tends to be more active, shaping how you interact with the world. In the realm of the Enneagram, everyone has two wings adjacent to their core type. However, one wing usually asserts its influence more prominently, much like how most people favour their right or left hand for complex tasks.

Helen Palmer, a respected name in the Enneagram community, emphasizes the importance of recognizing this dominant wing. According to her, it's not just an add-on but a lens that sharpens our understanding of an individual's unique persona. This is not a solitary viewpoint but echoes the collective wisdom of seasoned Enneagram practitioners. They hold that by getting to know your dominant wing, you gain a more nuanced understanding of yourself, somewhat like peeling an onion one layer at a time to get to the core. What's interesting is how this dominant wing modifies the characteristics of your core type. For instance, let's look at Type Seven, popularly known as the Enthusiast. If you are a Type Seven with a Six-wing (the Loyalist), you may display signs of being more grounded and security-oriented than a typical Seven. On the other hand, a Seven with an Eight-wing (the Challenger) could be more assertive, possibly displaying an adventurous streak that wants to break the mould.

Understanding the dominant wing can also be immensely helpful in relationships, both personal and professional. When you know your dominant wing, you can understand why you gel well with certain types and clash with others. It's almost like knowing the spices in a dish, which helps you figure out why it tastes a particular way. This sort of understanding can be crucial for team dynamics in the workplace or harmony in a household. A leader who understands the dominant wings of their team members can tailor their approach to get the best out of everyone, like a skilled chef who knows just the right amount of spices to add for the perfect dish.

Lastly, acknowledging the dominant wing doesn't just stop at self-awareness; it invites us into a journey of personal growth. If you are aware of how your dominant wing influences your actions, you can make more informed choices. For example, if you are a Type Four (the Individualist) with a Five-wing (the Investigator), you might notice a tendency towards introspection. Recognizing this can help you balance your introspective nature with the need for external engagement, creating a more well-rounded personality.

Wings in Action: Personal Growth and Wholeness

Understanding ourselves is like participating in a marathon where every checkpoint offers new insights. In the realm of the Enneagram, one such significant checkpoint is the concept of "wings". These wings, as elucidated by prominent Enneagram experts like Beatrice Chestnut and Russ Hudson, are not mere add-ons but essential modifiers that fine-tune our core personality types. Beatrice Chestnut emphasizes that understanding these wings enhances key aspects of our life, such as emotional intelligence, communication skills, and empathy. For instance, if you identify as a Type 4, known as the Individualist, and you have a 5-wing, your core qualities of creativity and introspection are likely to be further honed by the analytical tendencies typical of Type 5. This combination not only enriches your self-awareness but also equips you with a refined toolkit for navigating relationships with better understanding and harmony.

The emphasis on wings isn't a whimsical addendum to Enneagram theory. Experts like Russ Hudson stress that acknowledging and integrating these wings into our understanding can lead to a balanced and authentic life. It's akin to being proficient in both theory and practice in any given field, rendering you not just competent but exceptional. This notion finds resonance in the research conducted by Helen Palmer, who notes that as people mature, they often begin to manifest traits from their secondary or less dominant wing. This suggests a progression towards a more holistic, well-rounded personality. In essence, when you learn to integrate qualities from both your wings, you acquire the capability to express nuances and subtleties that you couldn't articulate before.

However, to truly benefit from this framework, one needs to invest time and effort into identifying not just one's core type but also understanding the impact and influence of the adjacent wings. While several tools and tests like the Riso-Hudson Enneagram Type Indicator serve as valuable starting points, it's crucial to recognize that these instruments can only provide initial guidance. The real depth of understanding is attained through consistent introspection and keen observation of oneself in various life situations over an extended period. In doing so, the study of Enneagram wings offers us not just a nuanced understanding of ourselves but also a more empathetic perspective towards others. It transforms our engagement with the world by helping us know not just the 'what' but also the 'why' and 'how' of our personalities. This understanding holds the promise of not just individual growth but also contributes to creating a harmonious, enriched collective existence.

Wings as a Symphony of Growth

In the journey of self-understanding through the Enneagram, the concept of wings serves as an indispensable guide that takes us beyond the surface of our core types. Just like a lead instrument in a symphony needs the accompaniment of other instruments to bring out a full-bodied sound, our core Enneagram types require the nuance brought by wings to manifest our personalities in a more complete manner. The insights provided by eminent figures in the field of Enneagram studies, like Riso, Hudson, Palmer, and Chestnut, have cemented the idea that these wings aren't mere additives; they are integral elements that offer a layered understanding of human personalities. Each of these experts underscores the role of wings in enriching the primary traits of the core types, thereby adding texture and complexity to our individual psychological profiles.

Moving to the practical implications, it becomes evident that understanding the concept of wings has a far-reaching impact, especially in the way we manage our personal and professional relationships. The wings, if properly understood and integrated, serve as harmonious notes that amplify and fine-tune the melody played by your core type. Take, for example, a Type 4, which is often seen as the Individualist. A dominant 5-wing would add analytical and observational strengths to the emotional depth of Type 4. Recognizing this and learning how to adapt these traits into everyday scenarios can lead to a more fruitful path of self-discovery and personal growth, enriching both your self-awareness and your interactions with the world around you.

While it's common to have one dominant wing that harmonizes with your core type, it's important to note that as we move through different life stages and accumulate more experiences, the lesser dominant wing also begins to assert itself. This gradual integration of both wings into our personality signifies a maturing, well-rounded individual. It is in this holistic approach that we find the symphony of our existence, a well-coordinated blend of core type and wings that not only deepens our self-understanding but also enriches our life experiences.

So, in essence, the Enneagram is not a static model but a dynamic roadmap, complete with its system of core types and wings. It beckons you to explore the different layers of your personality, encouraging you to understand the subtleties that make you uniquely you. This journey of self-exploration is not just an academic exercise but a transformative experience that allows you to create your own complex symphony of existence.

✱✱✱

Chapter Six

Enneagram and inter-relationships

Arrows and the Path of Integration

A rrows in the Enneagram system are akin to road signs in our journey of self-discovery. They guide us to certain paths under varying circumstances, directing us either towards growth or showing us where we might falter under stress. While the core Enneagram type is your home base, these arrows indicate routes towards two other types that influence your behaviour and personality in a profound way. Understanding the mechanism of these arrows provides a more nuanced picture of how we function and adapt in different life scenarios.

Consider a Type 1, commonly known as 'The Perfectionist'. This individual has the tendency to evolve by adopting qualities of a Type 7, who is 'The Enthusiast'. Under positive conditions, our Type 1 would find themselves exploring new interests and embracing spontaneity, breaking free from the shackles of rigidity. Conversely, when faced with challenges or stress, the same individual may gravitate towards characteristics of a Type 4, labelled 'The Individualist', where their behaviour could become more emotionally charged and focused inwardly.

To fully grasp this dynamic, it's crucial to look at the Enneagram diagram itself. Arrows connect your core type to these other two types, forming almost a triangular connection. One arrow leads you towards a type that

49

reveals your inherent stress responses, and the other one guides you to a type representing your optimal path for personal growth. In essence, these arrows serve as pointers for understanding not just who you are, but also how you can develop or how you might react when you're not at your best. These arrows, therefore, don't merely illustrate your traits; they narrate the unfolding story of your personal evolution.

Arrows act as a balancing act

Arrows introduce a balancing act between your core type, stress type, and growth type. While your core type remains your foundation, understanding your reactions under stress and your potential for growth offers a comprehensive view of your Enneagram journey. It's like navigating through life with an adaptable compass that guides you through various situations. Over the course of its development, there has been a nuanced evolution in the interpretation of these lines and arrows. Initially, a simplified perspective emerged, suggesting a dichotomy between "good" and "bad" arrows, corresponding to growth and stress movements. However, a more comprehensive understanding has since emerged, highlighting the significance of embracing both directions of movement for holistic personal development.

At its inception, the Enneagram's arrows were perceived as indicators of progress. Moving along the "good" arrow was believed to signify growth, while traversing the "bad" arrow represented disintegration. This interpretation contributed to a view of integration as a desirable state and disintegration as a hindrance to personal development. Consequently, this perspective created a dichotomy that oversimplified the intricate processes that occur within each individual's Enneagram journey. But it's now understood that both arrow points provide valuable expansions for each personality type, fostering a balanced and well-rounded individual. Instead of a linear progression towards growth and away from stress, the Enneagram recognizes the need for a holistic approach that incorporates both directions.

Enneagram and inter-relationships

Arrows introduce a compelling dance of balance among the core type, stress type, and growth type. The core type serves as the foundation, representing an individual's fundamental personality traits and tendencies. The stress type captures the way an individual responds under pressure, while the growth type embodies the aspirational qualities that one can integrate into their persona. This interplay creates a rich tapestry of traits and behaviours that reflect the complexity of human nature.

Navigating the Enneagram journey is akin to wielding an adaptable compass. The compass doesn't merely point in one direction; it dynamically adjusts to various landscapes, guiding one through different terrains. Similarly, the Enneagram's arrows offer a multifaceted guide through life's diverse situations, allowing individuals to draw upon both growth and stress aspects as they encounter challenges and opportunities.

Directions of Growth and Stress

In the Enneagram system, each personality type has a unique pattern of growth and stress. These patterns are often referred to as the "direction of growth" and the "direction of stress". They describe how individuals of each type might behave when they are moving towards personal development (integration) or when they are under increased stress (disintegration). Understanding these patterns can offer valuable insights into how individuals of different types might react and behave in various situations.

Direction of Growth (Integration)

The notion of Integration or "Direction of Growth" has garnered substantial attention from renowned Enneagram experts. They argue that Integration is a mechanism where you imbibe positive attributes from another specific Enneagram type, directly connected to your core type on the model's geometric layout. This process isn't arbitrary but follows a structured pattern that leads to more well-rounded human development.

For instance, if we talk about Type Two, which is widely referred to as the "Helper", these individuals are naturally geared towards providing support and care. However, as Don Riso and Russ Hudson have pointed out in their works, when a Type Two integrates, they acquire positive elements from Type Four, known as the "Individualist". It's like adding new shades to their emotional palette. They continue to be empathetic but also imbibe higher levels of self-awareness and creativity. This enrichment allows them to not just be caregivers but also individuals attuned to their deeper selves.

On a similar note, Type Nine, often termed the "Peacemaker", has its own unique journey. Helen Palmer's studies suggest that when Nines integrate, they assimilate traits from Type Three, the "Achiever". This integration doesn't derail them from their basic easy-going nature. Instead, it arms them with newfound focus, assertiveness, and a goal-oriented mindset. It's akin to adding more arrows to their quiver, allowing them greater flexibility in navigating life's challenges while retaining their inherent peaceful disposition. Integration is not about replacing one's core traits but augmenting them.

It doesn't dilute your original self but amplifies it, adding new layers of skills and perspectives. In this transformative journey, the Enneagram serves not just as a mirror reflecting your existing traits but also as a compass, indicating directions for meaningful personal growth. And according to these seasoned visionaries in the field, this is precisely what makes the Enneagram an indispensable guide in the quest for a more balanced, authentic self.

Direction of Stress (Disintegration)

The term "Disintegration" or "Direction of Stress" is crucial in the Enneagram model, extensively studied by scholars like Beatrice Chestnut and Claudio Naranjo. When an individual is stressed, they tend to adopt negative traits of another Enneagram type. This other type is located opposite their core type on the Enneagram triangle.

Take Type Five, the "Investigator". Typically, they like solitude and deep thinking. But when stressed, they show negative traits of Type Seven, known as the "Enthusiast". They might start to lose focus, jumping from one interest to another, essentially becoming a jack of all trades but master of none. Beatrice Chestnut's research suggests that this change can derail a Type Five's usual focus and drive them into counterproductive activities. Then there's Type Eight, the "Challenger", who are generally assertive and proactive. Stress pushes them towards characteristics of Type Five. Unlike their usual outgoing nature, they become withdrawn and overly analytical. Claudio Naranjo points out that this retreat can be a coping mechanism, a sort of mental bunker where they hide to strategize their next moves.

The knowledge of Disintegration is valuable for two reasons. First, it helps people understand their negative behaviours under stress, providing them a chance for timely self-correction. Chestnut's studies show that this awareness alone can often mitigate the adverse effects of stress. Second, as Naranjo argues, this understanding fosters empathy in interpersonal relationships. You become better at recognizing not just your stress points but those of others as well.

So, the study of Disintegration, along with its opposite, Integration, forms a comprehensive framework for personal development. It's not just about knowing how to grow, but also understanding what behaviours to avoid. This dual knowledge base, validated by experts in the field, serves as a comprehensive guide for both self-improvement and enhanced social interaction.

Utilizing Arrows for Self-Reflection

Understanding the arrows in the Enneagram system goes beyond mere academic interest; it serves as an actionable toolset for both personal and professional growth. The pioneers like Don Richard Riso and Russ Hudson have emphasized the transformative power of understanding arrows. Their theories suggest that these arrows serve as a comprehensive roadmap to navigate the complexities of human psychology. Understanding arrows means delving into our coping mechanisms during periods of stress and growth. And this understanding is not a solo journey; it extends its benefits to those around us. In the context of personal relationships, the arrows bring in a layer of empathetic understanding that is often missing in day-to-day interactions. Imagine engaging with a friend or a spouse and recognizing the tell-tale signs of their stress behaviour. It helps you pause and approach the situation with a more informed perspective. This isn't just about avoiding misunderstandings; it is about enriching the fabric of the relationship by inserting a nuanced understanding into it.

Taking this understanding into the workplace can be revolutionary, especially in leadership roles. Companies like the Enneagram Institute have leveraged this system to create holistic leadership training programs. The notion is straightforward but impactful: A leader aware of their team's stress and growth patterns is better equipped to manage challenges and foster an environment conducive to genuine progress. This leader can allocate tasks that align not just with the team members' skills but also with their psychological well-being. The arrows, therefore, become an invaluable asset in crafting a work culture rooted in empathy and tailored growth opportunities.

The application of Enneagram arrows is even broader when we consider social interactions in general. Social intelligence—knowing how to act or react in varied social settings—can be dramatically improved by understanding these arrows. When you're aware of someone's stress and growth arrows, you're less likely to misinterpret their actions, and you become more adaptable in your dealings with them.

✳✳✳

Chapter Seven

Embracing Redemption

The Journey of Redeemed and Unredeemed Enneagram Types

In the Enneagram, the idea of redemption is an eye-opener. It makes us realize that human personality is not set in stone, that it can evolve. The idea is straightforward: people can change, not just a little, but in ways that matter. So, let's talk about this concept of 'redemption' without any high-sounding words or convoluted theories.

When we refer to an 'unredeemed' type in the context of the Enneagram, what we mean is a personality still caught up in its own limitations. These are traits, behaviours, or attitudes that hold us back in some way. It could be an excessive need for approval from others, or a tendency to be overly critical, or a habit of procrastinating important tasks. Whatever form it takes, the 'unredeemed' aspect is something that doesn't help us live our lives to the fullest. It limits our growth, keeps us stuck in familiar but unhelpful patterns, and sometimes even causes us problems in our relationships and careers.

So, what happens when an 'unredeemed' trait becomes 'redeemed'? First of all, it doesn't mean the trait disappears or turns into its exact opposite. Rather, it evolves into a form that serves us better. For example, a person who's overly critical might become discerning instead. They would still notice details others might miss, but instead of just pointing out what's wrong, they might also see solutions and opportunities for improvement.

The journey from unredeemed to redeemed is a bit like cleaning a cluttered room. At first, you might feel overwhelmed by the mess. But as you sort through it piece by piece, deciding what to keep, what to throw away, and what to rearrange, the room starts to take on a new form. In a similar way, the process of redeeming one's traits involves some honest self-examination. It asks us to look at aspects of ourselves we might prefer to ignore or avoid, to hold them up to the light and see them for what they are. It's only by doing this that we can start to understand how these traits could be transformed into something more useful, more positive.

And how does one embark on this journey of redemption? First, by becoming aware of one's unredeemed traits. This can happen in many ways: through self-reflection, through feedback from others, or even through a crisis that makes you realize something needs to change. Once you're aware of what needs redeeming, the next step is to understand it deeply. This means asking questions like: Why do I behave this way? What fears or desires are driving this trait? What would happen if I acted differently? Once you have a good grasp of the 'why', the path to 'how' becomes clearer. Often, the journey involves replacing old, unhelpful behaviours with new, healthier ones. This isn't easy and takes time, but it's definitely possible. Tools like mindfulness, cognitive behavioural techniques, and even simple practices like journaling can be really helpful here. The aim is to make the redeemed trait a new habit, so deeply ingrained that it becomes a natural part of who you are.

So, why bother with all this? The answer is simple: redeeming your traits leads to a fuller, happier life. It allows you to engage with the world in a more authentic way, to build better relationships, and to find more satisfaction in your work. It helps you grow as a person. And that's something we all want, isn't it? The concept of redemption in the Enneagram gives us a framework to improve and grow. It teaches us that the aspects of our personality that hold us back aren't immutable. They can be understood, transformed, and even turned into strengths. This is a powerful message, one that opens up new possibilities for human growth and happiness. It's a message worth taking to heart.

The Redemption Journey: A Path to Wholeness

The journey toward redemption within the Enneagram framework is an exploration worth undertaking. It begins, as most journeys do, with acknowledgment. To avoid addressing one's unredeemed traits is to empower them further, allowing them to operate from the unconscious corners of one's personality. After acknowledgment, which serves as the entrance gate to this quest, we come face to face with the concept of self-awareness. It's not merely about introspection but about actively dissecting your thoughts, behaviours, and emotions to uncover what fuels them. For a Type 1, who is naturally inclined towards perfectionism and an acute sense of right and wrong, it's about probing deeper to find the underlying need for order and control. Do they stem from a childhood memory or an innate desire for social approval? It's about connecting the dots to form a coherent understanding of oneself.

Now that you know why your unredeemed traits exist, what's next? The path of redemption offers no shortcuts; instead, it demands rigorous practices, fine-tuned to individual needs. Consider cognitive-behavioural therapy, a strategy that's been immensely useful in dealing with problematic thought patterns. A Type 8, who might exhibit dominating tendencies, can benefit from this form of therapy to understand how they can wield their innate leadership skills without overshadowing others. But sometimes, our emotional obstacles are so deeply entrenched that they manifest as physical blockages in the body. This is where practices like yoga can be beneficial. For example, a Type 9, known for their peace-loving demeanour, might suppress their emotions to avoid conflicts, leading to bodily stress. Yoga, in such instances, helps in releasing this suppressed emotional tension.

Therapy is just one side of the coin; the other is continuous monitoring and assessment. An effective tool for this is journaling. Keeping a daily record not only provides a space to jot down emotions and experiences but also serves as a reliable method to observe changes, patterns, and transformations. Regular journal entries help in actively tracking the course of one's journey toward redemption. Here, a Type 3, who might be overly focused on accomplishments, can trace back their tendencies to seek validation from external achievements and reassess their values and goals.

While the role of experts in the realm of the Enneagram cannot be overstated, it's equally critical to engage in relationships that foster growth. Meaningful relationships act as mirrors reflecting both the good and bad, thus aiding in self-assessment. A Type 5, who often detaches from emotional realities, can gain immensely from such relationships, which challenge them to be more present and connected. These relationships become catalysts for change, pushing you out of your comfort zones, questioning your actions, and compelling you to grow.

It's crucial to mention that while the process involves constant action and assessment, it also requires its share of inaction—of stillness. The hustle and bustle of everyday life can sometimes drown the inner voices that guide you on this path. Regular intervals of quietude, where one can hear the whispers of their inner selves, become crucial in maintaining the balance and ensuring you're headed in the right direction. For example, a Type 7, eager for newer experiences, may find immense value in sitting still and reflecting, a practice that offers its own unique kind of richness.

However, one needs to understand that this path is not linear. It's a continuous process that requires regular introspection and realignment. The journey might feature relapses into older, unredeemed states, and that's perfectly acceptable. What counts is the ability to recognize such relapses and the resilience to return to the path. Thus, the journey from being unredeemed to redeemed within the Enneagram is far from an easy endeavour. It demands a high level of self-awareness, the implementation of various tools and strategies, and an enduring commitment to personal growth.

The journey toward redemption in the Enneagram framework demands a multi-pronged approach: acknowledgment, understanding, active change through therapies and mindfulness, regular assessments, and learning both from experts and personal relationships. It's a balanced blend of action and introspection, of hustle and pause.

While the road is arduous and long, the end result is nothing short of life-altering—a harmonious existence where you are the most authentic version of yourself, aligning closely with the virtues that characterize the healthier aspects of your Enneagram type. And therein lies the most fantastic aspect of this journey; it allows you to not just function but flourish, fully embracing the myriad dimensions of your complex, unique self.

Recognizing the Signs of Redemption

Embarking on the path of redemption is akin to stepping into a labyrinth of self-exploration, a complex maze with twists and turns that require extraordinary effort to navigate. The atmosphere is often murky at the outset, shrouded in a mix of uncertainty and anticipation. But it's not a journey one undertakes blindly; there are signposts, or markers, that illuminate the path.

The first such signpost is a heightened sense of self-awareness. When you understand the automatic triggers, fears, and defence mechanisms that have been dictating your actions, it's as if a blindfold has been lifted. Now, you have the gift of sight, of seeing yourself with newfound clarity. For instance, a Type 6 in the Enneagram, typically driven by a need for security, gains the ability to discern the difference between a genuinely threatening scenario and an illusion created by their inherent fears. And it's not just about gaining awareness; it's about understanding what this awareness means for your journey. It offers a pivotal moment to pause and reflect, a point where you recognize you have a choice in how you respond to situations, effectively breaking the chain of unconscious patterns.

This moment of clarity soon leads to the next milestone—willingness. Willingness to delve into the shadowy corners of your psyche and confront the fears and insecurities you've long avoided or denied. This willingness marks the next phase of the journey, taking courage and commitment to both acknowledge and understand why these fears exist in the first place. Let's consider a Type 8, known for their need for control; they may suddenly find themselves examining the vulnerabilities they had long swept under the carpet.

This sort of courageous exploration is indeed a testament to an individual's commitment to personal growth and transformation. It involves leaning into discomfort, embracing vulnerabilities, and untangling the emotional and psychological knots that have held you back. But confronting one's fears isn't the endgame; it's a process, one that begins to sow the seeds of another crucial signpost along the path—self-compassion.

As you delve deeper into understanding your Enneagram type and confront the fears that come with it, a newfound form of self-compassion starts to take root. You begin to see that these traits aren't flaws or inadequacies but rather integral parts of your complex human personality. For instance, a Type 9, who is often overly accommodating to avoid conflicts, may find this self-compassion allowing them to balance their natural inclination for peace with a newfound ability to assert their own needs and desires. This compassion then not only changes the way you view yourself but extends outwards, changing the nature of your relationships and connections with the world.

Moving beyond self-compassion, the virtues associated with your Enneagram type become increasingly evident, serving as guiding stars on this transformative journey. Take a Type 1, the Reformer, who may begin to move from an insatiable quest for perfection to a more balanced view that includes patience and acceptance. Likewise, a Type 4 could shift their focus from self-absorption to cultivating empathy and selflessness. These virtues act as beacons, signalling your transformation from who you were to who you are becoming. They are indicators of how far you've come, but also reminders that the journey is far from over. Redemption is not a finite destination but a continuous journey.

Thus, the Enneagram serves as a sort of roadmap. But it's essential to remember that while it illuminates the path, it doesn't provide shortcuts or easy ways out. Instead, it offers a comprehensive guide to traverse the complex landscape of your inner world, full of both challenges and rewards. In this endless journey, each step you take towards redemption makes you more authentically yourself, enriching not just your life but also the lives of those you interact with. The journey of redemption through the lens of the

Enneagram is hence not a solitary one but a collective human experience, an ongoing exploration of the vast terrains of the human psyche.

Practical Steps Toward Redemption

When you take up the journey of redemption through the Enneagram, it's a bit like deciding to climb a mountain. You know the climb won't be easy. The rocks underfoot are uneven, and the path ahead is unclear. You've got to be brave to even start, but you know that the view from the top—that sense of personal growth and improved relationships—will be worth every strenuous step. So, you pull yourself together and put one foot in front of the other. The Enneagram is like your trekking guide on this journey, showing you how to navigate through your own internal terrains.

Now, if you're going to get anywhere, the first thing you need is a good sense of direction. That's your self-awareness. You've got to know your own habits and tendencies, the things you do without even thinking. It's like recognizing that you always favour one leg when you climb. If you keep doing that, you'll tire yourself out before you get far. So, you turn to mindfulness practices. This can be as simple as taking a deep breath when something upsets you, just to give yourself a moment to think before reacting. It's like pausing to catch your breath on a steep climb. You can also read books on the Enneagram or attend workshops, which is a bit like having a guide shout out directions as you navigate tricky terrain.

The next step is about your relationships with others. Imagine you're climbing with a group. You can't just focus on your own path; you have to think about how you're interacting with your fellow climbers. If you notice one of them struggling, you wouldn't just pass them by, would you? Understanding that we all have our shortcomings, our unredeemed aspects, makes it easier to offer a hand or an encouraging word. It's not just about climbing your own mountain but helping others along their way.

As you keep climbing, each step aligned with the virtues like strength or wisdom that are naturally a part of who you are, something remarkable happens. The closer you get to the peak, the less you find yourself tripping over those rocks or stumbling on those roots. Your true self starts to shine through, lighting up your path. It reminds me of a saying by Carl Jung: when you look inside, you wake up. It's like reaching a point in your climb where the path suddenly becomes clear and you know, you just know, you're going to make it to the top. And that's the beauty of this whole journey. The Enneagram isn't just some roadmap; it's a compass for your soul. It shows you how to live more consciously, to be better not just for yourself but for everyone around you. It offers you a way to break free from your old habits and become who you were always meant to be. So, you climb, step by step, knowing that each footfall takes you closer to a better, more authentic life.

Chapter Eight

A Journey of Self-Discovery

Exploring your Enneagram type

Embarking on the journey of self-discovery with the Enneagram is like finding a guidebook to your own life. Your first step in this enlightening path is usually an Enneagram test. Although it's a valuable starting point, don't mistake the test results as the final word on who you are. These tests give you a snapshot, an initial outline that sketches the broader contours of your personality. They are efficient and can quickly point you in the direction you may want to explore further. However, the tests can sometimes focus only on the traits that are easy to see and miss out on the deeper aspects of your character. It's common to misunderstand a question and end up with results that don't quite fit.

After you've got some initial insights from the test, your journey takes you deeper into your own mind and heart. Think of this as the main section of your exploration, where you don't just skim the surface but dive deep. How do you react when you're stressed or how you behave when you're genuinely happy can reveal a lot about your type. It's a complex but very fulfilling process that will make you confront the different layers of your personality to finally get to its core. Along the way, you'll need to keep an open mind. Letting go of preconceived ideas about yourself is crucial. People tend to carry labels and stick them onto themselves; it's human nature. We've been classified by our families, friends, and even strangers since we were young. But here, it's essential to understand that the Enneagram is a dynamic tool that gives you the freedom to explore your personality without any constraints.

As you progress in this process, self-reflection becomes key. It's akin to piecing together a puzzle where each thought, each emotion, and each action is a piece that fits into the bigger picture. It's almost like being a detective of your own life. It may sound complicated, but it's incredibly rewarding. In the middle of this journey, you'll encounter the driving force behind your actions. Each Enneagram type has a core motivation that shapes their decisions. It's like the engine room of a ship, the place from where everything is powered. It could be a need for security, a desire for recognition, or a quest for knowledge. This driving force is the key that will help you understand not only yourself but how you relate to the world around you. It's important to also focus on your behavioural patterns. How you interact with others, how you react to challenges, and even how you celebrate joys can give you tremendous insights into your personality. It adds another layer to your understanding, not just about your motives but also about how those motives translate into actions in the real world.

But this is not just about the present; it's also about looking back at your past. Our early years, our upbringing, the environment we were raised in, all of these factors leave a lasting impact on us. It's like a handprint on wet cement; even if the cement hardens, the imprint remains. And so, a trip down memory lane, revisiting your childhood experiences, will offer you valuable clues to understanding your Enneagram type better.

Stress and growth are the two other essential aspects you need to consider. Stress can distort your personality traits and make you act out of character, while moments of growth can bring out the best in you. The dynamic interplay between these two aspects can offer you further clarity about your type. You don't have to walk this path alone. Experts in the field of Enneagram studies can offer you guidance. They've helped others navigate this complex but rewarding journey, and their insights can be invaluable.

Finally, blend all of this together—your test results, your self-reflection, and the advice from experts—to get a comprehensive understanding of your

Enneagram type. It's like making a multi-layered dish, where each ingredient enhances the others.

At the end of this journey, what you find is a deeper, more nuanced understanding of who you are. It's not just about sticking a number to your name. The Enneagram is much more than that. It's about embracing the complexities that make you uniquely you. And isn't that worth exploring?

A Word Before The Test

Enneagram tests have gained popularity as a means of self-exploration and understanding one's personality traits and tendencies. These assessments aim to identify an individual's Enneagram type among the nine basic personality types, each represented on the Enneagram symbol with its unique set of characteristics and attributes. By answering a series of questions or statements honestly, test-takers can gain a better understanding of their core personality type.

There are several leading Enneagram tests recognized for their accuracy and depth. One prominent option is the Riso-Hudson Enneagram Type Indicator (RHETI), developed by Don Richard Riso and Russ Hudson. This test is highly regarded for its comprehensive assessment of Enneagram types. It not only provides your primary type but also offers insights into your wings and levels of development. Another well-known test is the Enneagram Institute Test, also created by Riso and Hudson. It's widely accessible, with a free version available online, making it an excellent starting point for beginners. It introduces individuals to the nine Enneagram types, allowing them to begin their Enneagram journey without feeling overwhelmed. Additionally, the Integrative Enneagram Questionnaire (IEQ) stands out for its applications in the business world. It offers insights into how Enneagram types manifest in professional settings, making it suitable for those interested in personal and professional growth.

For newcomers to the Enneagram, the Enneagram Institute Test is often recommended. Its user-friendly interface and straightforward questions make it an ideal starting point. It provides a fundamental understanding of the nine personality types, allowing beginners to embark on their Enneagram journey without feeling overwhelmed.

Enneagram tests offer several advantages as tools for self-discovery and personal growth. One of the most significant benefits is enhanced self-awareness. By identifying their Enneagram type, individuals gain a deeper understanding of their motivations, fears, and behaviours. This heightened self-awareness can serve as a catalyst for personal growth and transformation. Moreover, the Enneagram is not limited to self-discovery; it also sheds light on interpersonal dynamics. Understanding the Enneagram types of others can lead to more compassionate and effective communication, enriching relationships.

Armed with knowledge of their Enneagram type, individuals can work on their weaknesses and leverage their strengths. It offers a roadmap for personal development and growth, allowing individuals to strive towards becoming the best versions of themselves. Furthermore, the Enneagram can be a valuable tool in resolving conflicts. By helping individuals recognize their triggers and responses in challenging situations, it fosters better conflict resolution strategies, contributing to healthier relationships.

However, Enneagram tests are not without their limitations. One significant drawback is their subjectivity. Enneagram typing relies on self-assessment, which can be subjective. Individuals may mistype themselves or resist their true type due to denial or a lack of self-awareness. Additionally, the Enneagram system can appear complex, especially for newcomers. Some may find it challenging to navigate the nuances of the nine types, their wings, instincts, and levels of development. Moreover, the Enneagram lacks extensive scientific validation, unlike some other personality assessments. While it has a rich history and anecdotal evidence of its efficacy, it may not satisfy those seeking empirical proof. Critics also argue that the Enneagram's descriptions of personality types can be overly generalized and may not capture the full complexity of human behaviour.

Enneagram tests serve as valuable tools for self-discovery and personal growth, offering individuals insights into their core personality traits and behaviours. They provide a path to enhanced self-awareness, improved relationships, personal development, and conflict resolution. However, it's essential to be mindful of their limitations, including subjectivity, complexity, limited scientific validation, and potential overgeneralization. The value of Enneagram tests lies in how individuals interpret and apply their insights to their unique journey of self-discovery and personal growth.

Now What?

Carl Jung, the great Swiss psychologist, once shared a profound thought, "Until you make the unconscious conscious, it will direct your life, and you will call it fate". Indeed, the Enneagram framework is a powerful tool to make this unconscious world a bit more accessible to us. It guides us to reflect on ourselves, understand our patterns, and leads us towards a journey of self-realization. Let's explore some practical ways to enrich this journey further.

Understanding Subtypes - Within each Enneagram type, you'll find three subtypes: self-preservation, social, and one-to-one. If you identify as a particular type, say Type 2 (the Helper), then understanding your subtype can tell you what you value most. Is it personal security, social relationships, or intense personal connections? Knowing your subtype can help you address your specific needs and make sense of why you behave the way you do.

Daily Journaling - Writing down your thoughts, feelings, and daily experiences is more than a pastime. It helps you see recurring patterns in your life. For example, if you write that you felt angry three times in one week and each time it was because someone interrupted you, then you know that's a trigger point for you. This way, you can find ways to deal with it better next time.

Mindfulness Techniques - Just paying attention to the here and now can teach you a lot about yourself. Start with just five minutes of mindfulness a day. Focus on your breathing or any current activity, be it eating or walking.

This helps you become aware of your immediate feelings and reactions, and it can teach you self-control.

Understanding Your Dreams - Keep a notebook near your bed and jot down whatever you dream as soon as you wake up. Review this dream journal every week. You might start to see certain themes or images that repeat. These recurring elements can give you a glimpse into what worries you, what excites you, and even what you desire deep down.

Feedback from Others - Ask people who know you well what they observe about your habits, mood, and reactions. Sometimes, a second perspective can reveal blind spots. But do remember, don't just accept what they say as the truth. Use their observations as additional information to understand yourself better.

Learning About Your Wings - In the Enneagram, the number next to your core type is known as your 'wing'. For example, if you're a Type 8, then your wings would be Type 7 and Type 9. Your wing can influence your core type in subtle ways. So, it's good to read up about these adjacent types to get a fuller understanding of your own type.

Attending Workshops - Workshops are like short courses where experts break down complex topics into simple lessons. If you attend an Enneagram workshop, you can ask questions, engage in activities and even meet others like you. It's an excellent way to quickly understand this framework and how you fit into it.

Visualization Exercises - Close your eyes and imagine yourself in different situations. Think about how you'd react. Afterward, reflect on why you felt that way. Doing this regularly helps you understand your emotional triggers, your stress points, and even what makes you truly happy.

Enneagram Panels - Sometimes, groups of people organize discussions where they talk about their experiences with their Enneagram types. Listening to these discussions can help you understand how different types react to similar situations. This is very useful if you are still not sure about your own type.

Seeking Expert Guidance - If you want a more structured way to use Enneagram for self-improvement, consider talking to a professional. They have the experience to guide you through this journey, helping you avoid common mistakes and offering tailored advice based on your type.

That's it—your comprehensive guide to diving deeper into understanding yourself through the Enneagram. The journey of self-discovery is long but always rewarding. Take it one step at a time. After all, the more you know yourself, the better you can navigate the ups and downs of life. The Enneagram serves as a constant companion on your journey through life, a guide for navigating the complexities of your inner world.

Far from pigeonholing you into rigid categories, it opens up avenues for self-discovery and personal growth. Remember, this tool is as dynamic and evolving as you are, adapting itself to your changing circumstances and understandings. It's crucial to approach it with an open heart and a curious mind, as these attitudes will enrich your journey. Not only does the Enneagram help you understand your unique traits, but it also allows you to build bridges of empathy and compassion with others.

It teaches us that understanding oneself is the first step to understanding the world, turning self-awareness into a gateway for more meaningful connections. Don't rush the process; be patient and allow yourself the space to grow and evolve. Be willing to revisit and question your insights periodically. The ultimate aim of engaging with the Enneagram is to lead a life that is not just self-aware but also fulfilling in its interactions with others. So continue this exploration, for with each step, you'll find your understanding of yourself and others deepening, making life's journey that much more rewarding.

Chapter Nine

Enneagram Types

What are they all about?

After having an understanding of the foundational principles of the Enneagram, we now arrive at the heart of our journey—the distinct Enneagram types that encapsulate the diverse spectrum of human behaviour and emotion. Each type is like a unique room in a grand mansion of human experience, holding its own set of stories, struggles, and strengths. As we step into each of these rooms, you'll find reflections of yourself and insights into others, sharpening your tools for personal growth and interpersonal understanding. So, let's turn the knob and walk into this enlightening chapter, keen to unravel the characteristics that make each Enneagram type not just unique, but also universally relatable.

Type 1: The Reformer.

Type 1 individuals in the Enneagram system can best be described as seekers of an ideal, ethical existence. For them, life is not just a series of events but a platform to demonstrate their deeply-rooted principles. Their core motivation is anchored in a persistent quest for excellence and correctness, a sort of life mission that they feel compelled to carry out. This drive stems from an inner moral compass that doesn't just guide them but, in a way, dictates their interactions with the world. The question of right and wrong isn't just philosophical pondering for them; it's a lived reality, shaping their everyday choices. The interesting aspect here is that the same internal compass that acts as their guide also serves as their inner critic. While they may appear self-assured, Type 1s often grapple with the fear of making a mistake or being immoral. The well-known Enneagram expert Russ Hudson emphasizes this, pointing out their underlying worry about being fundamentally flawed in some way. This fear keeps them in a state of heightened alertness, especially when it comes to moral and ethical choices, ensuring they stay true to their principles.

Discipline, a keen sense of responsibility, and an unwavering commitment to the task at hand characterize Type 1s in all facets of life. This could be in their professional commitments, in their personal relationships, or even in how they engage in self-reflection and personal growth. Such is their commitment to structure that they feel at ease in environments where rules and order are well-established. In essence, they are the backbone of any organized system, reliable and dependable, almost as if the organization would crumble without their steady support. These individuals aren't just responsible; they're also remarkably organized, almost to a fault. This facet of their personality often finds them in roles that require rigorous attention to detail, precise execution, and a disciplined approach. Whether they're engineers, teachers, or administrators, they excel in situations where their natural inclination toward meticulous planning and execution can shine.

However, like all personality types, Type 1s also have their vulnerabilities, most apparent when stress looms on the horizon. The high ideals they hold can morph into the breeding ground for self-criticism and external judgment under stressful conditions. The same standards that they strive to maintain can turn into a source of anxiety, making them increasingly harsh critics of themselves and, often, of others around them. This shift is not just subtle; it's significant enough to change the dynamics of their interpersonal relationships and professional engagements. Their inability to switch off this internal critic makes life increasingly difficult, not just for them but also for those who come into their sphere of influence. The crucial point, according to Enneagram literature, is that stress makes them susceptible to a loss of joy and relaxation, pulling them away from their innate zest for life.

One way out of this critical loop for Type 1s lies in the practice of self-compassion. It sounds simple but can be profoundly transformative. Learning to balance their inherent drive for excellence with an acceptance of human imperfections is the key to their growth. The moment they embrace this balanced perspective, the weight of always having to be perfect begins to lift, making room for a more accepting, tolerant disposition. This is especially important when you consider how their behaviour is often nuanced by adjacent Enneagram types, notably Type 2 (The Helper) and Type 9 (The Peacemaker). These adjacent types introduce an additional layer of complexity, adding to the rich tapestry of their already intricate personalities.

On the path of growth and transformation, the integration process leads Type 1s towards embodying the positive qualities of Type 7 (The Enthusiast). This integration makes them more receptive to life's varied experiences, more spontaneous and ultimately more joyful. In contrast, disintegration draws them closer to the negative traits of Type 4 (The Individualist), instigating mood swings and increased emotional sensitivity. But despite these ups and downs, the core of a Type 1's personality remains rooted in their yearning for a principled and orderly world. Their approach to conflict resolution is direct and rational, always anchored by their deep-seated commitment to fairness and justice.

In conclusion, Type 1s are compelling figures, motivated by an unwavering commitment to their principles and values. As they mature, their focus shifts from a self-centred quest for personal perfection to a more inclusive vision that seeks to uplift others. They evolve to become pillars of their communities, driving positive change and inspiring others to aspire for higher ethical standards. Their life journey is not just a personal quest but a collective endeavour, contributing to the greater good. So, studying Type 1 individuals offers a window into the dynamics of moral integrity and ethical conduct, qualities that have far-reaching implications for personal and social transformation.

Type 2: The Helper.

Type 2 individuals within the Enneagram framework are natural caregivers, defined by their intrinsic urge to help and support others. They operate on a kind of emotional radar, keenly aware of the needs and feelings of people around them. It's as if they are hardwired to sense emotional vacuums and are compelled to fill them. This nurturing disposition stems from a deep-rooted need for love and appreciation. The underlying principle guiding their actions is the belief that love is not an entitlement but something that has to be continually earned. The fear of being unloved or overlooked can often drive them to become exceptionally proactive in relationships, attending to the needs of others even before they are articulated. For them, the well-being of those they care about serves as a kind of mirror that reflects their own worth and validates their actions.

Type 2 personalities are exceptional emotional tuners. They can dial into people's feelings with acute sensitivity, offering empathy and understanding. Their listening skills are often highlighted as one of their strongest traits, making them not just effective communicators but also excellent nurturers. This acute sense of emotional awareness ensures that they are almost always in sync with the people around them, creating environments that are emotionally enriching and supportive. For Type 2s, this isn't just a skill set; it is an almost existential calling, a defining aspect of their identity. However, it's not all roses for these caregiver personalities. When faced with stress or emotional turmoil, the qualities that make them cherished friends and companions can recede, allowing less favourable traits to emerge. The need to be indispensable in the lives of others could push them into behaviours that are overly possessive or even manipulative. The fear of being unloved intensifies, and the result is a heightened focus on winning approval and attention, even at the cost of personal balance and emotional health.

The roadmap to personal growth for Type 2s involves an internal journey towards self-awareness. Their inclination to put others first must be tempered with the realization that their own needs and desires also warrant attention.

This involves setting emotional boundaries, an exercise that allows them to engage in self-care without feeling guilty about it. A more mature and self-aware Type 2 finds the golden balance between caring for others and self-nurturing, thus contributing positively to their own lives as well as those of others. Adding layers to the personality of a Type 2 are influences from adjacent Enneagram types. If you're a Type 2 but also find shades of Type 1, the Reformer, or Type 3, the Achiever, in your behaviour, that's quite natural. These influences contribute additional dimensions to the core traits of the Type 2, moulding them into unique individuals with complex but incredibly rich personalities.

In the professional sphere, Type 2 personalities are naturally drawn to roles that involve direct engagement with people, roles where their emotional acumen can be effectively utilized. Careers in counselling, healthcare, and social work are common pathways. Not only do these professions allow Type 2s to fulfil their innate need to be helpful, but their disposition also makes them particularly effective in these roles. Their co-workers and colleagues often view them as invaluable team members, known for building relationships founded on mutual respect and emotional support. The epitome of growth for a Type 2 individual comes when they transcend the need for external validation altogether. This level of emotional maturity allows them to give without expecting anything in return. They realize that love and affection are not commodities to be traded but gifts to be freely given and received. This newfound freedom manifests as an uninhibited flow of compassion and kindness, not just towards others but also towards themselves. In reaching this state, they embody the purest form of love and kindness, inspiring everyone around them to elevate their own standards of humanity and compassion.

So, in summary, the journey of a Type 2 individual in the Enneagram framework is a fascinating study of the human need for love and connection, set against the backdrop of emotional complexities and personal growth. Their pathway is about learning how to balance their genuine desire to nurture and be nurtured, and in doing so, they serve as a lesson to us all on the transformative power of love, empathy, and genuine human connection.

Type 3: The Achiever.

The Enneagram Type 3 personality presents an intriguing study in contrasts. Fundamentally driven by the need for success and recognition, these individuals are endowed with skills that make them naturally proficient in goal-setting. They pursue their objectives with tireless diligence, never letting up until they achieve what they set out to do. Complementing their work ethic is their social intelligence, which is quite remarkable. They are adept at networking and possess the ability to adjust their personas to fit into various social and professional settings. Yet, this pursuit for external markers of success conceals an underlying vulnerability—a pervasive fear of failure and feelings of unworthiness. One of the most well-documented traits about this personality type is how their sense of self-worth is intricately tied to their accomplishments and the approval they receive from their social circle. This phenomenon has been underlined extensively in Enneagram studies, which focus on the need of Type 3s to gauge their value based on external achievements.

Stress and its associated challenges form an inevitable part of the life journey for Type 3 individuals. When they find themselves in stressful situations, their already competitive nature can intensify to levels that may be perceived as overbearing. This is driven by an almost insatiable urge for external validation, a craving so overpowering that it can overshadow the individual's other positive attributes. This single-minded focus on success and the approval of others can result in a form of emotional emptiness that settles deep within them, even when they appear to be successful by societal standards. This paradox, an emotional void despite a veneer of success, has been a focal point in academic discourse concerning this Enneagram type.

Personal growth for Type 3 personalities is not just a process but a journey—a complex journey at that. It's a path toward acknowledging their value, which exists independent of any laurels they may have won or any acclaim they have received. This journey of self-discovery is often enriched by the influences from adjacent Enneagram types, specifically Type 2, which is called the Helper, and Type 4, known as the Individualist. These influences do more than just add facets to their existing traits. They provide depth, adding complex layers to their motivations and behaviours, which in turn can either enrich or complicate their lives, depending on how they are managed.

Another significant aspect to consider in the developmental journey of Type 3 individuals is the concept of integration. They stand to gain considerably from incorporating positive attributes of another Enneagram type—Type 6, known as the Loyalist. Integrating these traits can make a world of difference as it nurtures a sense of deep trust in themselves and in their relationships with others. This is crucial for their mental and emotional well-being and provides an inner security that may have eluded them earlier. But it's not a one-way street. The process of disintegration poses its own set of risks, as they may start adopting negative traits from Type 9, also called the Peacemaker. Such a state of disintegration can make them lose touch with their own true desires and ambitions, leading to an existential crisis of sorts.

Conflict resolution is another domain where Type 3s display a unique approach. While they remain goal-oriented in most aspects of their lives, the way they manage conflicts is no exception. Their strategies are usually framed with well-defined objectives, but the journey of personal growth involves an added layer of complexity. It brings the challenge of separating their sense of self-worth from their accomplishments and involves them embracing their authentic emotions and values. This not only broadens their emotional spectrum but also equips them with the ability to resolve conflicts in a way that is both balanced and emotionally fulfilling.

So, what does a well-rounded, mature Type 3 individual look like? They are people who have successfully learned to align their intense drive for success with their true, authentic selves. No longer are they purely driven by what society expects of them or what external rewards they can amass. They have grown attuned to their own unique needs and desires, contributing to a holistic approach to both their personal and professional lives. This transformation is profound and has been emphasized in scholarly works as a defining feature of an emotionally and psychologically mature Type 3 individual.

The Heart Centre of the Enneagram, which comprises Types 2, 3, and 4, is primarily associated with emotional responses and interpersonal relationships. It brings into focus qualities like empathy, desire, and authenticity. For Type 3s, their positioning within this centre underscores the importance of balancing their impressive list of achievements with their internal emotional and psychological needs. Achieving this delicate balance is central to their quest for personal growth and forms the core of their journey toward becoming well-rounded individuals who are not just successful but also emotionally fulfilled.

In their most evolved form, Type 3 personalities embody an alignment that goes beyond the superficial. Their goals and ambitions are no longer merely items on a checklist but resonate deeply with who they are at their core. This alignment is transformative and enables them to live life in a manner that is both fulfilling and authentic. The scholarly literature on this subject frequently accentuates the intricate balance between ambition and genuine self-expression as a defining feature of a mature Type 3 individual.

Type 4: The Individualist

Type 4 on the Enneagram is known as the Individualist, and the name captures the essence well. These are people deeply interested in understanding themselves and the world around them. They are like explorers of the human experience, always keen to dig deeper into their feelings and thoughts. What drives them mainly is a search for authenticity and the urge to express themselves in a way that stands apart from the norm. They often have this motto running at the back of their minds: "I am different, unique, and destined for something extraordinary". This belief fuels their aspiration to carve out an identity that is distinctly their own.

People often notice that Type 4s have a remarkable emotional depth. They are skilled at navigating the complicated maze of human emotions. You might say their mind is like a rich library of feelings, where even the most complex sentiments find a place. This emotional wealth not only helps them appreciate art, music, and literature but also contributes to their ability to connect with these forms of creative expression.

If you're looking for real-world examples, consider celebrities like Johnny Depp and J.K. Rowling. Depp's choice of diverse movie roles and unconventional fashion styles is a testament to his pursuit of unique self-expression, very much in line with what we understand about Type 4s. Type 4s are known for their creativity, individualism, and emotional depth. Rowling's imaginative world-building in the Harry Potter series, as well as her own personal journey from struggling single mom to one of the world's most successful authors, captures the essence of this type quite well.

However, life isn't always a smooth sail for Type 4s, especially when stress comes into the picture. The qualities that make them exceptional can also become their Achilles' heel. Their penchant for deep introspection can turn into an excessive self-focus, almost like they're getting lost inside themselves. Likewise, their quest for something extraordinary can sometimes lead them to feel isolated from the rest of the world. Studies in the Enneagram field have pointed out that Type 4s often feel like something crucial is missing in their lives. This sense of absence fuels a never-ending search, leading to mood swings and periods of sadness.

The path to personal growth for a Type 4 involves a delicate balance. On one hand, they need to celebrate their unique qualities; on the other, they must find joy in everyday life. Part of this journey includes self-acceptance, recognizing that their value isn't just tied to their distinct traits but also to their genuine selves. This realization can be quite liberating, as it opens them up to finding happiness in the simple things in life.

Type 4 personalities also become more complex when influenced by neighbouring types on the Enneagram wheel. A Type 4 with traits leaning toward Type 3, known as the Achiever, might channel their creativity into more practical forms. They could be more focused on achieving tangible success, whether in the workplace or in artistic fields. On the flip side, if a Type 4 takes on characteristics of Type 5, called the Investigator, their journey could lean towards scholarly or introspective pursuits. They might engage in academic research or deep studies to understand themselves and the world around them.

In a mature state, the Type 4 personality finds a harmonious balance between individuality and universal human experiences. No longer burdened by a perpetual sense of inadequacy or an obsessive need for uniqueness, they learn to find value both in what sets them apart and what they share with others. This shift enables them to engage with the world in a more balanced way, transforming their deep emotional currents from a source of angst to a wellspring of empathy and connection. Additionally, the redeemed Type 4 is more pragmatic in their pursuits, often incorporating positive traits from adjacent Enneagram types. For instance, qualities from Type 3 can infuse practicality into their creative endeavours, while aspects of Type 5 can deepen their introspective journey, making them seekers as well as finders of wisdom. The mature Type 4 evolves from being a restless soul forever searching for something elusive to becoming a balanced individual. They appreciate life in all its complexities, finding meaning both in what makes them unique and what connects them to the broader tapestry of human experience. This transformation doesn't just enrich their own lives, but also makes them emotionally insightful companions, capable of adding depth and meaning to the lives of others.

Type 5: The Investigator

In the Enneagram system, Type 5 personalities stand out as voracious seekers of knowledge and wisdom. Driven by an insatiable curiosity, they are the ones diving into books, theories, and intricate studies, all in an attempt to decode the world that surrounds them. Figures like Albert Einstein and Bill Gates exemplify this archetype. Einstein's ground-breaking work in physics set the stage for much of our modern understanding of the universe, illustrating the quintessential Type 5 drive to probe the boundaries of human knowledge. Rowling, with her detailed fictional world in the Harry Potter series, also showcases the Type 5's unrelenting commitment to understanding complex systems. Both luminaries show that when a Type 5 directs their intellectual pursuits constructively, the results can be nothing short of revolutionary.

However, this intense intellectual focus doesn't come without its pitfalls. Often, Type 5s prefer their own company to that of others, choosing to retreat into their internal worlds of logic and analysis. This tendency to be lone wolves can make it difficult for them to forge deep, meaningful relationships with other people. And when under stress, Type 5 personalities can double down on this isolation, focusing excessively on intellectual concerns and shunning emotional or social interaction. This becomes problematic in a world where emotional intelligence and relationship-building are often just as crucial for success and well-being as are technical skills and book smarts.

On the path of personal growth, the challenge for the Type 5 is to find a healthier equilibrium between their intellectual quests and their emotional lives. They have to understand that being well-rounded individuals involves not just cognitive pursuits but also emotional intelligence. Borrowing from traits of adjacent Enneagram types can prove beneficial here. Learning a bit from Type 4, for example, could bring some much-needed creativity and emotional depth to their logical approaches. Taking cues from Type 6 may add elements of loyalty and caution that could benefit them in personal and professional relationships. And when conflicts arise, they are usually adept at dissecting the issue logically. However, a fully mature Type 5 learns that life's problems can't always be solved through rational analysis alone; sometimes, a dash of empathy and emotional understanding is needed to arrive at truly effective solutions.

Redemption for a Type 5 comes when they begin to share their insights and wisdom, stepping out from the solitary confinement of their minds to make a meaningful impact on the world. They realize that their true value doesn't just lie in what they know but also in what they contribute. In this redeemed state, they find a harmonious balance between their inward journeys for knowledge and their outward expressions of wisdom. No longer just passive consumers of information, they become active contributors to the world's store of wisdom and understanding, enriching not just their own lives but also those of the people around them.

In summary, the journey of a Type 5 from an intellectual recluse to a wise sage is a fascinating one. It involves not only the accumulation of knowledge but also its meaningful application in various spheres of life, from personal relationships to broader societal impact. This enriches not only their own journey but also brings valuable perspectives and insights into the world at large.

Type 6: The Loyalist

In the Enneagram model, Type 6, commonly known as The Loyalist, is a captivating blend of vigilance and unwavering loyalty. Deeply rooted in a need for security and stability, Type 6 individuals navigate life with a constant eye out for safety and certainty. Their strong commitment to relationships and systems gives them a unique position in the social landscape. Think of that friend who's always there for you, no matter the situation. That's a quintessential Type 6. Public figures like the late Supreme Court Justice Ruth Bader Ginsburg and actor Tom Hanks offer excellent examples of this type. Ginsburg's long fight for justice and equality, as well as Hanks' warm and relatable on-screen personas, underscore the key attributes of Type 6: dedication, dependability, and a commitment to fostering a sense of security and belonging for all.

However, this intense focus on security has its drawbacks. When stressed or faced with uncertainties, Type 6 individuals often experience anxiety and worry. They can become consumed with imagining the worst-case scenarios or even doubt their own abilities and judgment. These mental tendencies often drive them to seek reassurance from external sources, showing their inherent vulnerability. The key challenge for Type 6 individuals is to cultivate a greater sense of self-trust and to realize that true security comes from within. Growth for them means acknowledging their own intuition and abilities, thereby emerging stronger, more self-assured, and resilient in the face of life's unpredictable challenges.

The Type 6 personality is also influenced by interactions with neighbouring Enneagram types like Type 5, The Investigator, and Type 7, The Enthusiast. Incorporating some of Type 5's analytical skills can make a Type 6 more thoughtful and intellectually curious. Conversely, drawing upon the adventurous spirit of Type 7 can make them more willing to embrace new and diverse experiences. As they integrate and evolve, they find a significant alignment with the positive characteristics of Type 9, The Peacemaker. This alignment facilitates a more balanced approach to life, allowing them to seek safety and security without succumbing to excessive worry or anxiety.

In moments of disintegration, however, they may find themselves displaying traits similar to Type 3, The Achiever, focusing too heavily on success and losing sight of their core need for stability. Conflict resolution for a Type 6 typically involves a keen awareness of group dynamics and a striving for consensus. However, they can augment their conflict-resolution approach by being more flexible and by learning to trust their own intuitive insights a bit more.

In their redeemed state, Type 6 personalities become powerful advocates for justice and change. Freed from the shackles of their anxieties, they stand up boldly for what they believe in, fostering an environment of trust and unity. Their focus shifts towards the well-being of the community at large, turning them into champions of fairness and empowerment. This transformative journey from caution to courage, from dependency to self-reliance, adds an invaluable layer of loyalty and dependability to any social fabric. In essence, a redeemed Type 6 not only becomes a strong pillar for themselves but also serves as a reliable cornerstone in the broader context of community and societal well-being.

Type 7: The Enthusiast

Type 7 in the Enneagram is often called The Enthusiast for good reasons. People of this type are filled with a zest for life, always eager to explore new things and experiences. They're the ones you'll find planning their next vacation while still on the current one, eager to squeeze every drop of joy out of life. This inherent optimism often becomes infectious, inspiring those around them to look on the brighter side of things. If you want to know what a Type 7 looks like, think of public figures like Jim Carrey. Their careers are testaments to a larger-than-life approach, where every opportunity for joy or learning is seized upon.

The guiding belief for Type 7s is simple: they want to be happy and fulfilled. This desire shapes their decisions, often propelling them toward activities that promise immediate gratification. Whether it's a thrilling outdoor activity, a captivating book, or an engaging conversation, Type 7s are there, ready to jump in. They often see a silver lining in every situation, making it easier for them to navigate life's ups and downs with an unwavering spirit.

However, it's not all sunshine and rainbows for the Type 7 individual. Their continuous search for new experiences can sometimes make them restless. When faced with stress or uncomfortable situations, they're likely to avoid the issue rather than confront it. This evasion can result in impulsive decisions and a tendency to shy away from addressing deeper emotional complexities. Therefore, the path for personal growth for Type 7 involves learning to be present and content in the moment, even if it doesn't offer immediate pleasure. Developing mindfulness and taking the time to explore their deeper emotions can lead them to a more balanced life. It can help them realize that not all joy comes from external experiences; some of it needs to be cultivated from within.

Interaction with other Enneagram types like Type 8 (The Challenger) or Type 6 (The Loyalist) often enriches the personality of a Type 7. Borrowing a bit of the assertiveness from Type 8, for instance, can result in a more focused and driven Type 7, without losing their sense of fun or adventure. On the other hand, the caution and loyalty seen in Type 6 can help Type 7s be a bit more circumspect, aiding them in assessing risks more effectively before diving headlong into new adventures.

As they evolve, Type 7s find that they share attributes with Type 5 (The Investigator). This helps them go beyond surface-level interests to explore subjects in depth, giving a more rounded quality to their quest for joy. But when things go south, they might display characteristics similar to Type 1 (The Reformer), becoming perfectionists and overly critical of themselves and others. In terms of conflict resolution, Type 7s are naturally skilled at finding out-of-the-box solutions. This unique approach often injects a sense of creativity into problem-solving situations. However, this skill can be further honed by practicing patience and active listening, which will help them not just find quick solutions but also long-lasting ones.

In their best form, Type 7s learn to direct their natural enthusiasm toward meaningful endeavours. Instead of merely seeking short-term gratification, they aspire for experiences that add value not only to their lives but also to those around them. Their journey transforms them from being pleasure-seekers to individuals who appreciate depth and significance, all the while maintaining their innate sense of enthusiasm and wonder. Thus, the story of the Type 7 individual is a journey from exuberance to wisdom, from being adventurers to becoming sagacious wanderers. By embracing both the highs and lows of life, by recognizing that even discomfort has something to teach, they come to embody a more mature form of enthusiasm—one that doesn't just uplift themselves, but also those fortunate enough to be in their orbit.

Type 8: The Dynamo

Type 8 personalities are naturally inclined towards leadership, carrying a no-nonsense attitude and a knack for taking charge. This makes them the kind of people who stand out, especially in challenging situations where decisive actions are needed. They are assertive and unyielding, qualities that generally command respect and attract followers. If you're looking for real-world examples, consider the lives of people like Lady Gaga who have demonstrated remarkable tenacity and unflinching resolve, navigating through the challenges and hurdles in the respective fields to reach the pinnacle. The common thread running through their life stories and those of many Type 8 individuals is a deep-seated belief in their own ability to control their destiny. They operate from a strong inner conviction that often drives them to fight for justice and what they believe is right.

However, this assertiveness and desire for control can also act as a double-edged sword. While these traits make them strong and confident, they can also escalate under stress, leading to strained relationships and conflicts. For Type 8 individuals, vulnerability is often seen as a sign of weakness, which is contrary to their belief system. Therefore, a significant part of their personal growth journey involves learning how to balance their inherent traits of assertiveness with qualities like empathy, openness, and even vulnerability. The challenge is to recognize that vulnerability is not a weakness but another form of strength that allows them to build deeper, more meaningful relationships. This balancing act is crucial for them to evolve into leaders who are not only strong but also sensitive and caring.

Type 8s also display a unique blend of characteristics when they interact with other Enneagram types. For instance, incorporating the compassionate and supportive qualities of Type 2 (The Helper) can make them more formidable yet caring leaders. This fusion results in a more effective leadership style, especially in roles that require strong interpersonal skills. On the other hand, influences from Type 5 (The Investigator) can add a layer of thoughtfulness and reflection to their decision-making processes. This added dimension helps in making them more rounded individuals who are not just focused on action but also on the implications of those actions. Through such interactions, they understand the importance of evolving by absorbing positive traits from other types, thus becoming better leaders and relationship-builders.

In conflict situations, Type 8 personalities are known for their confrontational approach. They are not the ones to avoid a problem; rather, they face it head-on and look for solutions. This can be both an asset and a liability. While their direct approach often helps in quickly resolving issues, it needs to be coupled with skills like active listening and compromise to be truly effective. As Type 8s continue on their personal growth journey, they learn to integrate these complementary skills. They understand that conflict resolution is not just about imposing one's will but involves building consensus and fostering a collaborative environment. Over time, as they evolve, their assertive traits are directed more towards empowering and safeguarding others rather than controlling them.

When Type 8 personalities reach a point of maturity or "redemption", as it is often called, they undergo a transformation that is quite remarkable. At this stage, their natural assertiveness and strength are harnessed for greater good, serving as tools for empowering those around them. No longer are they merely strong individuals fighting for their own place in the world; they become champions for justice, equality, and fairness. Their leadership takes on a nuanced form, driven by a renewed understanding that strength is most effective when used to uplift others. In a sense, they become guardians of their communities, using their formidable skills to foster an environment of dignity, respect, and mutual support. Their voice becomes the voice for those who cannot speak for themselves, and their strength becomes a protective shield for the vulnerable. In this redeemed state, Type 8 individuals serve as inspiring examples, showing that the path to true leadership and personal fulfilment lies in the balance of strength with empathy, control with compassion, and assertiveness with understanding.

In conclusion, Type 8 personalities are strong-willed and naturally inclined towards leadership roles. However, their journey is one of balance and integration, learning to channel their strengths in a way that allows them to build deeper connections and become more effective leaders. By embracing their inherent traits while also integrating qualities from other Enneagram types, they pave the way for a fulfilling life. They evolve from being just leaders to catalysts for positive change, inspiring others through their own journey of self-discovery and growth. This makes them not just strong individuals but also contributors to stronger, more resilient communities.

Type 9: The Peacemaker

Type 9 personalities, commonly referred to as Peacemakers, are individuals who aim to create a sense of harmony and unity in their environments. Their approach to life revolves around their deep-seated desire for peace, both internal and external. They have a knack for defusing tension, often serving as mediators in conflicts. These people are guided by their yearning for tranquillity, which influences all their actions and decisions. Notable figures like Nelson Mandela and Bob Marley epitomize this personality type. Mandela's role in reconciling a racially divided South Africa, and Marley's globally resonant music advocating for love and unity, are vivid illustrations of the impact Type 9s can make. While their drive for peace makes them exceptional mediators and nurturers of harmony, it can also pose challenges on the personal front. Often, their focus on external peace leads them to side-line their own needs and aspirations. In order to achieve a balance, they need to learn to assert their personal desires without compromising their natural peacefulness.

The interplay between Type 9 and other Enneagram types adds different shades to their personalities. When they come into contact with Type 1 personalities, known as The Reformers, they may adopt a more justice-oriented approach while maintaining their peaceful essence. Similarly, interactions with Type 6, The Loyalist, could make them more cautious and committed in their relationships. Regarding personal development, integration with traits from Type 3, The Achiever, can significantly help Type 9s become more proactive about their dreams and aspirations without losing their innate calmness. On the other hand, absorbing negative traits from Type 6 may induce states of anxiety and self-doubt, especially during stressful situations. Conflict resolution is a forte for Type 9s; they usually adopt a strategy of active listening and empathetic understanding to find a middle ground. With personal evolution, they can also become more assertive, voicing their own perspectives without destabilizing the peace they cherish.

In a mature or "redeemed" state, Type 9 personalities become even more effective as mediators and facilitators of peace. They manage to channel their inherent ability to understand multiple viewpoints into a proactive tool for conflict resolution. Their leadership style in this phase is not just about maintaining peace, but actively promoting it. They overcome their initial tendencies for self-neglect and complacency, taking assertive roles in fostering understanding and resolution among conflicting parties. Their balanced and evolved state shows that it's possible to be both peace-loving and assertively effective, thereby setting an example for others to emulate.

***

Let's wrap up!

Understanding the Enneagram is not just a journey of self-discovery but also a way to gain deep insights into the complexities of human behaviour. This knowledge goes beyond the personal realm. It can be a robust framework for improving social skills and relationships. It's essential to note that Enneagram is useful everywhere—not just in personal relationships but also in professional settings like offices and classrooms. When applied properly, it allows us to navigate team dynamics more effectively, thereby leading to better collaboration and an overall more productive work environment.

Leadership takes a new turn when looked at through the lens of the Enneagram. Traditional notions of leadership often focus on directive roles, but the Enneagram teaches us that understanding individual motivations is the key to effective leadership. This nuanced perspective allows us to tailor our approach, recognizing the unique strengths and inclinations of different personality types. Consequently, the teams we lead become more cohesive and innovative. It's about fostering an environment where each team member can realize their full potential, driving not just individual but collective success.

So, as we conclude our exploration of the Enneagram, it's crucial to recognize that this is just the beginning. The tool offers a lifelong framework for understanding not just ourselves but others too. The real value lies not merely in understanding these nine personality types but in applying this understanding in practical ways. It's about transforming our relationships and making a lasting impact, whether at home, work, or in broader society. The Enneagram isn't just a theoretical construct; it's a guide for living authentically, forging meaningful connections, and leading effectively. It provides a pathway for continued growth and learning, underlining the need to regularly revisit its principles to adapt to new situations and challenges.

Overall, the Enneagram serves as a dynamic tool for various aspects of life. It is not confined to introspection but extends to interpersonal relationships and professional development. With its practical applications in team dynamics and leadership styles, it proves itself as a multifaceted instrument for promoting individual and collective growth. In embracing the Enneagram, we embark on a journey not just of self-awareness but of understanding the world around us in a more nuanced manner. It's not a quick fix or a one-time assessment but a continuous process of adaptation and learning. Embracing the Enneagram principles equips us for a life of meaningful interactions, conscientious leadership, and ultimately, personal and societal transformation.

Chapter Ten

Numerology

A rich palette of different shades

I n the previous chapters, our primary focus has been on the Enneagram—a comprehensive system that draws from psychology, spirituality, and ethical philosophy to provide a detailed picture of human personality types. As we progress, the objective is to widen the lens and consider how the Enneagram resonates with or diverges from other numerological and astrological systems, specifically, Chaldean Numerology and Vedic Numerology. While the Enneagram offers an intricately woven psychological tapestry, these other systems add layers of meaning rooted in ancient wisdom, astrological concepts, and spiritual beliefs. By doing this, we aim to equip you with a multifaceted toolkit for self-exploration, with each tool offering its unique view on human nature and destiny.

Chaldean Numerology originates from ancient Babylonian civilization. It's a method of understanding human life by associating each letter in the alphabet with a number. For instance, the letter 'A' corresponds to the number 1, and the letter 'B' to 2, so on and so forth. The sum total of the numbers derived from a person's name is used to make predictions about various aspects of their life, including career, relationships, and health. In essence, Chaldean Numerology provides an astrological interpretation of human existence. It is less fluid and more deterministic compared to the Enneagram. Once your Chaldean numbers are calculated based on your name, they become somewhat like an immutable blueprint. Unlike the Enneagram, which accounts for shifts in personality types based on varying life circumstances, Chaldean Numerology largely regards your numerical representation as a stable entity, an almost unchanging guide to your life.

Vedic Numerology, on the other hand, is a distinct system deeply rooted in the spiritual and philosophical teachings of ancient India. The very word 'Vedic' is derived from the Sanskrit word 'Veda', which translates to 'knowledge'. This form of numerology is not just focused on numbers, but also incorporates the Hindu concepts of Dharma (duty), Artha (material prosperity), Kama (desire), and Moksha (liberation). Unlike Chaldean Numerology, which is largely astrological, and unlike the Enneagram, which is predominantly psychological, Vedic Numerology fuses ethical and spiritual dimensions into its numerical representations. Here, each number is a guidepost for moral, ethical, and spiritual behaviour. These numbers are believed to have a deeper connection with cosmic vibrations and are even thought to be influenced by planetary positions. Vedic Numerology encompasses a vast range of life experiences; it can guide decisions related to marriage, career choices, and even the best times to undertake new endeavours.

In the comparison of these systems, the advantage lies not in elevating one over the others but in understanding the unique strengths and perspectives each brings to the table. The Enneagram provides a nuanced psychological analysis of human behaviour, Chaldean Numerology offers a more deterministic and astrological viewpoint, while Vedic Numerology adds a spiritual and ethical layer, richly influenced by ancient Indian philosophy. Each system offers insights that are valuable, each contributes to a fuller, more complex understanding of human nature and the world we inhabit.

As we transition from a detailed discussion on the Enneagram to a comparative study involving Chaldean and Vedic Numerology, we aim to offer a comprehensive narrative. In the following chapters, we will delve deeper into the Chaldean and Vedic systems, discussing their historical roots, methodologies, interpretations, and modern applications. Our ultimate goal is to offer you a broad set of perspectives and tools for self-exploration and understanding. Think of each system as a different lens in a telescope; each lens offers a different magnification, a unique field of view, and when these lenses are combined, they enable us to see a much larger, more detailed picture of the cosmos, and consequently, of ourselves.

Therefore, as we venture further into this multifaceted journey of human understanding through numbers, let's appreciate the diverse lenses available to us. By comprehending the unique aspects and contributions of each system—Enneagram, Chaldean Numerology, and Vedic Numerology—we are better equipped to explore the complexities and marvels of human existence. This sets the stage for a rich, interconnected narrative that we will continue to build upon as we delve into the heart of these ancient and modern systems, each offering unique insights that complement and enrich our collective wisdom.

Greek Influence

In the long history of human civilization, very few periods radiate as brightly as ancient Greece's enduring contributions to cosmic exploration, profound philosophical thought, and rigorous scientific investigation.

In ancient Greece, remarkable thinkers contributed significantly to the way we understand the world today. Among iconic landmarks like temples and marketplaces, great philosophers like Pythagoras, Plato, and Aristotle pushed the limits of human thought. They were constantly seeking to understand more, deeply curious and unwilling to settle for simple answers. They played a crucial role in establishing the methods of logical and scientific reasoning that have influenced human progress for centuries. Their work set the stage for various academic disciplines and philosophies that have made a lasting impact on human civilization.

In a setting highlighted by Ionic columns and marble structures that seem to reverberate with the wisdom of antiquity, Pythagoras presents an intriguing synthesis of the numerical and the divine. While he is best known for his contributions to mathematics, specifically the Pythagorean Theorem, his intellectual pursuits went far beyond math alone. Pythagoras believed that numbers had a deeper, almost spiritual meaning, not just a utility in calculations.

This unique viewpoint proposed that numbers were not just mathematical entities but were deeply connected to the spiritual aspects of existence. Numbers, in his view, had a role beyond solving equations; they could also offer insights into the mysteries of the cosmos. This idea gave rise to what is now known as Greek numerology—a study linking numbers to a broader understanding of life and the universe. Pythagoras' approach had a lasting impact, not just in mathematics but also in the realm of philosophy. His ideas invited future scholars to explore the overlap between math and metaphysics. In doing so, he set a foundation for various branches of intellectual exploration that continue to influence academic thought today. His contributions extend from providing a new understanding of numbers to also expanding the scope of philosophical inquiry. As a result, Pythagoras remains a cornerstone figure for multiple academic disciplines, drawing sustained interest from scholars keen to explore the depth of his inter-disciplinary thought.

In ancient Greece, figures like Hipparchus and Ptolemy were much more than astronomers; they were seekers keen on unravelling the universe's mysteries. They used intricate models to explain the complex movements of celestial bodies. But their work did more than just map the night sky. It helped bridge the gap between the mathematical and the mystical, laying the groundwork for Greek numerology to evolve. Pythagorean Numerology, an extension of this ancient thought, was shaped and polished by Pythagoras' intellectual successors. In this system, numbers took on a new dimension. Far from being mere tools for calculation, they were imbued with deeper, spiritual significance. They were seen as guides to understanding the very fabric of existence. The Pythagorean Table was central to this. This enigmatic chart, often attributed to the followers of Pythagoras, went beyond just numbers. It made connections between numerical values and symbolic meanings, drawing upon elements of mythology and spiritual concepts.

So, while astronomers like Hipparchus and Ptolemy began by peering into the night sky, their legacy reached far beyond astronomy. Their pioneering work fostered an intellectual atmosphere that allowed for the fusion of math and philosophy, leading to compelling numerological systems that continue to intrigue us to this day.

In Greek philosophy, the quest for self-realization held a significant place. The Delphic maxim "Know Thyself" wasn't just a poetic phrase; it was an invitation to explore one's inner psyche, resonating well with the cosmic order that the Greeks believed in. The principle aligns closely with the modern psychological tool known as the Enneagram. This system offers a detailed map of human personality types, grounded in basic motivations, fears, and aspirations. It aims to guide individuals in understanding themselves better, much like the ancient Greek philosophers who sought alignment with cosmic principles.

Egyptian influence

The story of Egyptian civilization is not just a chronicle of kings and wars; it's also a narrative of numbers and meanings. When we look at Egypt, we don't just see pyramids and temples, we see a civilization that valued numbers not only for commerce and engineering but also for their deeper, almost mystical meanings. This thinking mirrors the principles of the Enneagram, a modern personality mapping system, revealing that humans have long been fascinated by the spiritual dimensions of numbers.

The Great Pyramid of Giza is an architectural wonder, but it's more than that. It represents the Egyptian interest in celestial alignments. This interest in the sky and what lies beyond resonates with the Enneagram's attempt to understand human personality traits and their relation to broader cosmic truths. Cheiro, a figure who was influential in popularizing numerology, argued that numbers have unique vibrations that could provide insights into one's personality and fate. This concept isn't new; it has its roots in ancient civilizations like Egypt, which ascribed metaphysical meanings to numbers.

Ancient Egyptians were some of the early adopters of numerology, a field that sees numbers as more than mere symbols for counting. They believed numbers connected the earthly world with the divine, something echoed by later thinkers like Pythagoras. This Greek philosopher, who spent nearly two decades in Egypt, considered numbers to be elements of a divine language that explains the world's order. This line of thinking continued well into the era of St. Augustine, who also believed that numbers were a divine gift to help humanity understand the world. So, when we look at the Enneagram, we shouldn't just see a modern framework, but a continuation of a long-standing human attempt to derive deeper insights from numbers.

In Egyptian culture, numbers were often embedded in religious and philosophical contexts. They calculated areas, solved equations, and their understanding of geometric shapes was surprisingly advanced. For example, the Egyptians had a grasp of how to calculate the pyramid's slope long before Pythagoras formalized his theorem. And it's not just about practicality. In the Karnak Temple Complex, named 'Apet-sut', which means 'Enumerator of the Places', we see the symbolic importance given to numbers. The numbers 2, 3, 4, and 7 had a special, almost sacred status in Egyptian numerology, representing a variety of natural and cosmic orders.

For Egyptians, the numbers 2 and 3 were foundational. They saw the world as based on dual principles, which could be either masculine or feminine. The goddess Isis represented the feminine principle and was associated with the number 2. Osiris, her male counterpart, was linked with the number 3. These numbers were seen as the building blocks of the universe, overseeing all phenomena. Writers like Plutarch and Diodorus of Sicily later confirmed this idea, reinforcing the symbolic importance of 2 and 3 in Egyptian culture. These numbers had specific attributes and were associated with qualities of the sun, wisdom, and destiny. The numbers 2 and 3 also played a significant role in Egyptian myths, such as the story of Isis and Osiris. When these two deities united, they gave birth to Horus, who was associated with the number 5. Horus embodied both the feminine and masculine qualities of his parents, representing a cosmic balance. This symbolizes the completion of a cosmic cycle, much like the Enneagram's ultimate goal of achieving a balanced personality. The idea that these numbers are deeply symbolic aligns with Ma'at, an ancient Egyptian concept symbolizing the fundamental order and balance of the universe.

Ancient Egyptian numerology is an enlightening field that adds another layer of depth to our understanding of this civilization. Numbers were not mere mathematical symbols; they were interwoven with religious, philosophical, and even cosmological views. These perspectives were not isolated; they influenced thinkers like Pythagoras and Augustine, and they resonate with modern frameworks like the Enneagram. While the Enneagram may not claim a direct lineage from Egyptian numerology, the focus on using numbers for deeper understanding is a common thread that ties human thought across cultures and eras. So, when we think about numbers, let's remember that they have had a long journey from the banks of the Nile to our modern charts, carrying with them the wisdom of ages. Their significance extends far beyond arithmetic, serving as keys to unlocking a richer understanding of the ancient Egyptian worldview.

Numerous insights into Egyptian culture have been lost to time, leaving us with a limited number of documents that explore Egyptian numerology and the meaning of numbers. Nonetheless, these fragments provide a tantalizing glimpse into the intricate ways numbers were woven into the fabric of ancient Egypt's worldview.

Kabbalah Numerology

Kabbalah Numerology finds its essence in the mystical teachings of Kabbalah, a vital facet of Jewish mysticism. At the heart of this system lies gematria, a practice wherein each Hebrew letter corresponds to a specific numerical value. This sacred correspondence unveils hidden meanings within words, embodying the Kabbalistic belief in the existence of profound layers of reality. The foundational principle of Kabbalah Numerology asserts that numbers possess profound spiritual significance, acting as bridges between the earthly and the divine. Each number is believed to resonate with distinct energies and qualities, thereby echoing the cosmic order that underpins the universe. This parallel echoes the Enneagram's exploration of distinct personality types and the vibrational interpretations of Chaldean Numerology.

Kabbalah Numerology employs gematria to meticulously analyse words, names, and phrases. Through calculating numerical values, practitioners gain insights into hidden meanings that may not be apparent at surface level. This methodology shares parallels with Chaldean Numerology, which similarly assigns numerical values to letters to unveil hidden insights. Such interconnectedness underscores the universality of numerological exploration, where various systems intersect to decode the complex encryption of existence.

While Kabbalah Numerology leaves its imprint on other systems, it retains its unique identity firmly rooted in Jewish mysticism. The Enneagram, while touched by Kabbalistic insights, maintains its foundational framework of nine personality types. Chaldean Numerology, influenced by Kabbalistic concepts, continues to honour its ancient Babylonian roots.

Chapter Eleven

Chaldean Numerology

Chaldean Numerology, a system of understanding life's complexities through numbers, has ancient origins, yet its wisdom is still sought today. Starting from the cradle of civilization in Mesopotamia, particularly in the intellectual haven of Babylon, this knowledge has travelled through ages and across cultures. The Babylonians weren't just concerned with the phenomena they could see. They extended their inquiry into the cosmic landscape, peering into the relationship between numbers and the universe. For them, each number held a unique vibration, a specific energy, intrinsically connected to the greater cosmic order.

The baton of this ancient wisdom was passed on to other great civilizations, and each absorbed it in its unique way. The Greeks, who already had a rich intellectual tradition, integrated Chaldean Numerology into their expansive philosophic discussions. When it reached the sands of Egypt, it met a civilization deeply rooted in symbolism and mystical traditions. India, with its Vedic practices and deep-rooted spirituality, saw a natural alignment between its beliefs and the principles of Chaldean Numerology.

The journey of this age-old wisdom might have lost its trajectory had it not been for individuals like Cheiro, born William John Warner. An Irishman who recognized that wisdom isn't confined to texts but lives within the practices of cultures, Cheiro set foot in India to delve deeper into this mysterious science. While he was an ardent student, he was also an excellent communicator. He moved in elite social circles, offering consultations to figures like Mark Twain and Oscar Wilde. He became the bridge between ancient wisdom and the modern world. Cheiro's skill lay in simplifying intricate theories and making them accessible to people far removed from the subject. Cheiro did not upend or radically change the principles of Chaldean Numerology; rather, he gave them a fresh vitality. He revived an almost forgotten wisdom, making it both relevant and comprehensible to contemporary minds. Cheiro made numerology accessible, but it was not watered down. It retained its core principles, which speak to a range of human experiences and needs.

One of the central principles in Chaldean Numerology is the concept of the Life Path Number, calculated from the date of birth. This number serves as a guiding light, providing insights into one's inherent traits, possible destiny, and life challenges. Importantly, this number isn't static; it is a dynamic component that evolves as one moves through various life stages. The Expression Number, calculated based on one's full name, is another critical element. This number outlines the social dynamics of a person, encapsulating how one engages with the world. While the Life Path Number looks inward, examining the person's essence, the Expression Number looks outward, focusing on how this essence manifests in social interactions.

In addition to individual analysis, Chaldean Numerology also introduces the concept of Karmic Lessons. These are essentially life lessons tied to specific numbers and act as guideposts for personal growth. They often reveal themselves at critical junctures in life, providing wisdom and guidance when one is at crossroads. Another dimension in this field is the concept of relational numerology. By comparing the Life Path Numbers and Expression Numbers of two individuals, one can glean insights into the interpersonal dynamics at play. It opens a new analytical avenue to understand the intricacies of human relationships, whether romantic, platonic, or professional.

Putting it all together, Chaldean Numerology is a comprehensive system of understanding the world and one's place in it. From the meticulous astronomers and mathematicians in Babylon to the deeply philosophical Greeks, from the symbolism-rich Egyptians to the spiritual Indians, each culture has contributed to this system's multifaceted nature. And then came figures like Cheiro, who breathed fresh life into it, modernizing its concepts without compromising its essence. Despite varying cultural contexts, all contributors to Chaldean Numerology share a common understanding—numbers are not mere symbols; they hold the key to deeper cosmic truths. Each culture, while applying its unique lens, has invariably focused on names, birth dates, and specific numbers as elemental to understanding life's complexities.

The Number System

In Chaldean numerology, each number takes on a persona of its own, with attributes that influence human lives in various ways. This age-old system has its roots in ancient civilizations, and it offers a comprehensive understanding of your life path, destiny, and more. To truly grasp this form of numerology, you have to know not just what these critical numbers are but also how to calculate them. So, let's get started.

1	2	3	4	5	6	7	8
A	B	C	D	E	U	O	F
I	K	G	M	H	V	Z	P
J	R	L	T	N	W		
Q		S		X			
Y							

Chaldean Numerology Alphabet Numbers

The Chaldean numerological alphabet system differs from Pythagoreans. Pythagorean numerology uses the number nine but Chaldean numerology has no number "9" in their calculations. The Chaldeans believed that the number nine had sacred and holy qualities and held it away from all other numbers. However, if your name equals "9", then the nine remains.

In contrast to the Pythagorean system, Chaldean numerology offers a distinct methodology that diverges in several key aspects. While Pythagorean numerology follows a straightforward alphabetical sequence, Chaldean assigns numbers to letters based on their vibrational qualities. This approach makes the Chaldean system more complex but also more nuanced, taking into account the specific energies and frequencies emitted by each letter. Another distinctive feature is that Chaldean numerology entertains the concept of name changes impacting one's destiny, which is generally not the case in the Pythagorean system. Lastly, Chaldean numerology often involves compound or double-digit numbers, unlike its Pythagorean counterpart that mainly focuses on reducing numbers to single digits, except for the recognized master numbers. These differences give each system its unique flavour and approach to unveiling the intricacies of one's life and destiny.

Destiny Number (Expression Number)

The Destiny Number is your life's blueprint. It casts light on the talents you're born with and the challenges you'll encounter. It steers your career choices, your relationships, and, in many ways, your ethical and spiritual orientation and acts like a guide to help you understand the directions your life might take. The Destiny number is also called Expression number, since this number influences what and how you express yourself in different stages and faces of your life. It uses your full name at birth to give you a number that can tell you about your strong points as well as the challenges you may encounter. Take careers as an example. If your Destiny Number turns out to be 3, it's very likely you'll be at ease in professions where communication is key. You may end up being a writer, a teacher, or even a radio host. These careers are all about expressing yourself, something that the number 3 is often associated with. But if your Destiny Number is an 8, you'll probably find that you're more suited for roles that require leadership and decision-making. You might be more at home in managerial positions where you can apply your natural knack for organization and control.

Your Destiny Number is derived from your full name. There are division amongst numerologists which name we should be availing for calculation. There is a school which suggests we should take the name as in the birth certificate as it is the name given to us at birth. But some prominent numerologists like Cheiro suggests to use the name we are known and called the most as it is the one has the most vibrational influence over us. And remember, even though the birth certificate name seems modern, the ancient cultures have given much importance in the naming ceremony of a child and usually its closely associated with religious and spiritual rituals. I suggest you could accept the method which seems more rationale as some cultures still give much importance to the name given at birth. And there is also a school which suggests that each name we use – like a pet name in the family, formal name at work, or the signing name in career – each have influence over those particular areas

In Chaldean numerology, each letter is assigned a specific numerical value between 1 and 8 (the number 9 is considered sacred and is generally omitted). These assignments are done based on the Aramaic language, which was spoken by the Chaldeans, but it has been modified for Roman based alphabets by experts like Cheiro.

To calculate your Destiny Number, first match each letter in your full name to its Chaldean number equivalent and then add them up. Reduce the sum to a single digit, except for the numbers 11, 22, and 33, which are considered Master Numbers.

For instance, if your name is John Doe, the calculation would go like this:

John: J(1) + O(7) + H(5) + N(5) = 18
Doe: D(4) + O(7) + E(5) = 16

Total: 18 + 16 = 34 which could be further reduced like 3 + 4 = **7**

Your Destiny Number also has something to say about how you approach relationships. If you're a 6, family and close relationships are probably at the heart of your life. You're likely to excel in jobs where you can take care of others, perhaps something in healthcare or education. This is because the number 6 usually points to a caring and nurturing nature. You may also find that you maintain long-term friendships and relationships because you are willing to put in the emotional work required. But if you are a 1, you are probably more focused on achieving your own goals and milestones. You may prefer a bit more independence and space to go after what you want.

To put it plainly, knowing your Destiny Number is like having a helpful hint or a nudge in certain directions in life. While it doesn't dictate what will happen, it offers insights into where you may naturally excel or what challenges you could face. With this information, you can make better decisions and maybe have a smoother ride through life's ups and downs.

Soul Urge Number

The Soul Urge Number, in essence, reveals the core of your emotional self, the undercurrents of your existence that might not always be visible on the surface but guide you nonetheless. This number isn't about the external face you show the world or your behavioural traits which the Destiny Number tells us, rather it's about what drives your soul and what makes the innermost part of you tick. This is the number that speaks volumes about your internal motivations, your true longings, and what you crave for deep within your soul to feel truly fulfilled.

The role of the Soul Urge Number is both subtle and profound. On a day-to-day level, it may influence the choices you make unconsciously, the things that seem attractive to you without you even understanding why. Yet, on a grander scale, it can set the tone for your entire life path. It's like the compass that you internally refer to when you make major life decisions—be it in love, career, or spiritual pursuits.

You see, a person can pursue a career for years, earn well, and gain all the societal badges of success but still feel unfulfilled if the job doesn't resonate with their Soul Urge Number. Imagine a person whose innermost desire is to nourish and nurture, being stuck in a job that's all about competition and personal achievement. The disharmony between the soul's urge and life circumstances can often lead to a sense of emptiness that's hard to explain. Similarly, in relationships, understanding your Soul Urge Number can be like deciphering a critical piece of a puzzle. It can help you understand why certain relationships, no matter how perfect they seem on paper, just don't give you the kind of emotional satisfaction you yearn for.

However, it's crucial to remember that the impact of your Soul Urge Number is not deterministic; it's not set in stone. Awareness is the first step towards transformation. Knowing what your soul is genuinely yearning for can empower you to make life choices that align better with your inner self. The influence of this number often becomes more palpable as you mature and grow into your own, mainly because as you age, your understanding deepens, and you become more in sync with your true self.

You become less willing to ignore the subtle but persistent pull of your Soul Urge Number. Your Soul Urge Number serves as a hidden guide, somewhat like a lighthouse, often unseen but always felt. It's that quiet voice in the midst of life's noise, nudging you towards choices that resonate with the deepest parts of your being. Listening to it might not always be easy, but those who do often find a sense of fulfilment that many spend a lifetime searching for.

In the Chaldean system, calculating the Soul Urge Number, also known as the Heart's Desire Number, involves a methodology that diverges from the Pythagorean approach. In the Chaldean system, each letter has a specific vibration and is assigned a numerical value between 1 and 8; the number 9 is considered sacred and is excluded from most calculations unless the final sum of a name results in 9. First, you'll need a chart that lists the Chaldean number assignments for each letter.

Unlike the Pythagorean system, the Chaldean system is not alphabetically ordered. To find your Soul Urge Number, you'll use your birth name—ignoring the consonants—and focus solely on the vowels. Assign the Chaldean numerical values to each vowel in your name and then add them together. If you arrive at a double-digit number, continue reducing it until you get a single digit. However, like in the Pythagorean system, if the number sums to a 'Master Number'—in Chaldean, these are often the numbers 11, 22, and sometimes 33—you would not reduce it further. For instance, if your name is 'Rohan', the vowels are 'O' and 'A', and their Chaldean values are 7 and 1 respectively. Adding 7 and 1, you get 8. So, your Soul Urge Number, according to the Chaldean system, would be 8.

Personality Number

In the Chaldean system of numerology, the Personality Number is a telling metric that lays out how you are generally perceived by the world. While it doesn't delve into your inner workings or core motivations, it's more like the facade of a house, revealing how people quickly judge or understand you based on initial interactions. This number is often viewed as the outward manifestation of yourself, what you show to others during casual encounters. In a way, it's the garment you wear in public, carefully chosen but not necessarily indicative of what lies beneath the fabric.

This is calculated by using the consonants in your full birth name. Each consonant is assigned a specific numerical value according to the Chaldean system. After calculating these numbers, they're summed up, and if it's a double-digit number, you keep reducing it to a single digit, unless it's a master number like 11, 22, or 33, which are usually left as they are.

The impact of the Personality Number is quite substantial when you look at social interactions. Whether you are at a job interview, a first date, or a social gathering, the impression you leave is often guided by this number. It can dictate the first layer of people's perception of you, shaping the immediate responses you get from them. This has a ripple effect on your social dynamics and even career opportunities. It's important to note that while the Personality Number may show the world a particular side of you, it's not an exhaustive revelation of your true self. But knowing it can provide a helpful understanding of how you can be more approachable or how you might appear to others. In essence, it can serve as a form of social navigation, making the journey of interpersonal relationships less turbulent and more harmonious. Bear in mind that this number alone does not define you; it merely provides a frame of reference. Your full numerological profile would comprise various other aspects like your Life Path, Destiny, and Soul Urge Numbers, which together create a more nuanced and in-depth view of your life's purpose, challenges, and gifts. Nonetheless, the Personality Number in the Chaldean system serves as an intriguing mirror reflecting how the world initially sees you.

Let's say your full birth name is "Anil Kumar Sharma". For calculating the Personality Number, we focus only on the consonants, which in this name are N, L, K, M, R, S, H, R, and M. In the Chaldean system, the values for these consonants might be N=5, L=3, K=2, M=4, R=2, S=3, H=5, R=2, M=4. Adding these together: 5+3+2+4+2+3+5+2+4 equals 30. You'd reduce the 30 to a single digit: 3+0 equals 3. Therefore, your Personality Number according to the Chaldean system would be 3.

Life Path Number

The Life Path Number is like a compass on the convoluted path of life, serving multiple roles to enrich your understanding of your own journey. It's a number that could influence your career trajectory, relationships, the challenges you'll face, and the innate talents you possess. For instance, if your Life Path Number is 5, you're likely to feel an inner pull toward careers that are dynamic and filled with change, steering clear of anything that might seem routine or monotonous. This magnetic push or pull is not just confined to career choices; it extends to your personal relationships as well. If you carry the qualities of a number 2—diplomacy and peace-making—you might find that you're naturally compatible with certain numbers and that your life seems to unfold more smoothly when aligned with compatible energies.

But life isn't all about comfort zones and compatibility. Each Life Path Number comes with its own set of hurdles and challenges, which aren't necessarily setbacks but rather lessons tailored for your personal growth. The number can shine a light on what obstacles are likely to come your way, helping you not to dread them but to anticipate and learn from them. Your Life Path Number can also act like a spotlight on a stage, highlighting your innate skills and talents. A number 1, often seen as a leader's number, might make you comfortable in taking charge and steering the ship, whether it's in a family setting, a workplace, or even among friends.

In the Chaldean system of numerology, calculating the Life Path Number usually revolves around your birth date, much like the Pythagorean system, but the interpretation and meaning can differ. Here's how you would go about calculating it - Firstly, you need to write down your full date of birth in a day-month-year format. Let's say you were born on the 25th of December 1985. In this case, the day is 25, the month is 12, and the year is 1985.

The next step is to reduce each component to a single-digit number by adding the individual digits together. In our example:

- Day: 25 is 2+5, which equals 7.

- Month: 12 is 1+2, which equals 3.

- Year: 1985 is 1+9+8+5, which equals 23.

We then reduce 23 further to a single digit, 2+3, which equals 5.

Once each component of the birth date is reduced to a single digit, you add them together: 7 (day) + 3 (month) + 5 (year) = 15.

Finally, if the sum isn't a single-digit number, you reduce it further to get a single-digit Life Path Number. In this example, 15 is 1+5, which gives us a Life Path Number of 6.

Calculating your Life Path Number offers you essential insights into your life's journey, the challenges you'll face, and the opportunities that lie ahead. Though this process may seem simple, it opens doors to a complex and intriguing set of values and interpretations that can guide you in various aspects of your life. Understanding your Life Path Number can also offer a soothing predictability in a world that is often chaotic and unpredictable. It gives you a broader framework within which you can make your choices. While it doesn't provide a minute-to-minute account of what's going to happen, it gives you enough of a general direction to help you navigate life's complexities. And that's one of its most invaluable offerings: the gift of insight and guidance. By understanding this number, you can walk through life with a little more confidence and a little less confusion, always having a touchstone to return to when you need to regain your sense of direction.

Maturity Number

In Chaldean numerology, the Maturity Number holds a special place, often regarded as a pivotal number that reveals itself more prominently as you age, usually around your middle years. This number is a glimpse into the inner you, throwing light on the person you will evolve into as years pass by, acting as a guiding light towards fulfilling your spiritual and personal objectives. The Maturity Number is like a distant beacon, not influencing your life much in the early years but becoming more significant as you grow older, illuminating paths you might not have considered before.

In the intricate tapestry of numbers that influence your life, the Maturity Number helps you understand the kind of wisdom or skills you'll acquire as you age. As you walk the path of life, there are challenges that mould you, experiences that enrich you, and this particular number gives you insights into the kind of transformation you'll undergo. It's akin to looking into a mirror that reflects not your face but your soul's aspirations, telling you what you'll most likely focus on in the latter part of your life. It fills in the gaps left by other numbers in your numerological profile, offering a more rounded view of your destiny. For instance, a person with a Maturity Number relating to leadership might not show these traits early in life but may find themselves naturally gravitating towards leadership roles as they age, even if their Life Path or Destiny Numbers suggest something else. The Maturity Number can also suggest latent talents or interests that become important later in life, often in ways that are harmonious with the individual's overall numerological chart. Say, if your other numbers incline you towards artistic pursuits, the Maturity Number might point towards a specific form of art that you'll embrace passionately after a certain age.

One of the most poignant features of the Maturity Number is its power to bring equilibrium to your life. It often harmonizes with the energies represented by other numbers in your profile. In this sense, it serves as an integrative force, helping to bring cohesiveness to your life's journey. So, even if your Life Path and Destiny Numbers represent divergent paths, the Maturity Number may act as a bridge between the two, uniting them in a common objective.

Decoding You

The emergence of the Maturity Number in your life, usually noticeable around the age of 50, is like receiving a burst of new energy that pushes you to refocus on what really matters to you. You begin to notice that you have less tolerance for wasting time on matters that don't align with your ultimate goal, whatever that might be in your individual case.

Calculating your Maturity Number is straightforward. You simply add your Life Path number to your Destiny or Expression number. Let's consider an example. If your Life Path number is 9 and your Destiny number is 5, you'd add them up: 9 + 5 equals 14, which in turn reduces to 5. Also worth noting in this example is the presence of a Karmic 14/5.

What's intriguing about your Maturity Number is how it fits—or doesn't fit—with the rest of your Numerology profile. There may be a sense of harmony or conflict between your Maturity Number and your other numbers, which can result in either a seamless journey or some challenges ahead. This mix of energies, whether it's smooth or contains friction, influences the trajectory of the latter part of your life.

✳✳✳

Chapter Twelve

The Chaldean Numbers

Chaldean numerology provides an incredibly nuanced way to understand human nature, emphasizing that there is no absolute good or bad number. Each comes with its own set of complexities, influenced by planetary energies, and offers unique lessons and challenges to those under its vibration. The idea is not just to understand these numbers, but to harmonize with them, to align oneself in a way that these energies serve as guides rather than hurdles on the path of life. Each number in Chaldean Numerology has a corresponding planetary influence, which adds another layer to its interpretation. As we dig deeper into the fascinating realm of Chaldean numerology, it becomes apparent that each number serves as a kind of mirror reflecting not just individual traits but also universal principles.

What each of these numbers represent in each of the life's numbers – Destiny, Life Path etc – is a much bigger topic to discuss, and much complex to master. It effectively overflows the capacity of this book, so hopefully another time we can discuss in detail about that. Here I am trying to give the nature of each number in general so that you can contemplate how it will affect each facets covered by those numbers.

The number 1 represents the essence of leadership and initiative, and it calls to mind the qualities of the Sun—full of energy, light, and a singular force that acts as the centre of a system. This number resonates with people who carry a certain dynamism that others find hard to ignore. People influenced by this number are frequently found in leadership positions, showcasing pioneering thoughts and actions. But like the Sun that can scorch if one gets too close, the drive to lead can sometimes border on arrogance or a tendency to dominate. The number 1, apart from its leadership qualities, is also associated with the drive for independence. This number often corresponds with a pioneering spirit, a keen intellect, and a knack for invention. People influenced by this number may also have a relentless pursuit of perfection, sometimes to their own detriment as it can lead to isolation or loneliness.

Next, the number 2 signifies the art of balance and duality. It stands as a counterpoint to the individualistic nature of 1 and brings to the forefront the qualities of empathy, cooperation, and harmony. It resonates with the lunar principle—the Moon that softly illuminates the night sky, serving as a partner to the harshness of the daytime sun. If 1 is about me, then 2 is about 'we'. This number often marks people who excel in partnership roles, whether in marriage, business, or any form of joint endeavour. While number 1 wants to lead, number 2 seeks to harmonize. As we deepen our understanding of the number 2, we find it also reflects a keen intuition. People influenced by this number often possess uncanny perceptiveness about others. They are gifted with a knack for peace-making and reconciliation. This can sometimes lead to them putting others' needs before their own, causing an imbalance in their personal lives.

The number 3 is an ode to the expansive, Jupiterian influence that it carries. This number symbolizes the power of communication, networking, and extension. People influenced by the number 3 are often found to be social butterflies, full of zest for life, and with a rather optimistic outlook. They possess the unique ability to uplift others, just as Jupiter's gravity affects its surrounding moons, encouraging them to shine brighter. But sometimes, this exuberance can manifest as superficiality or a lack of focus. The number 3, with its communicative flair, often carries a sense of humour and an ability to inspire. These individuals often have multiple talents and are adept at multitasking. However, this can also lead to a scattering of energies, as they might try to do too much at the same time, thereby diluting their effectiveness.

Number 4 is a tribute to solidity, much like the foundational strength of a well-constructed building. Under the watchful eye of Uranus, this number is pragmatic, focused, and exceptionally organized. Those under its influence are planners, the ones who build futures on concrete actions, rather than leaving things to chance. However, an overemphasis on order can make them resistant to the changes that life inevitably brings. The stability of number 4 also carries a stubborn streak. Individuals under this influence are often strong-willed and uncompromising, which can make them excellent in roles requiring focus and commitment. However, this determination can also manifest as inflexibility, making them less adaptable to change.

For those who resonate with the number 5, life is a thrilling ride under the swift Mercury's influence. They embody the essence of change, variety, and freedom. People influenced by this number are like Mercury, orbiting the Sun at an incredible speed, always in a hurry to experience the next big adventure. However, this constant pursuit of the new can sometimes make them fickle and unreliable. When we talk about number 5, its love for change also implies adaptability. These people are highly adaptable and can feel at home in almost any environment. This, however, can sometimes lead to a lack of rootedness or a feeling of being scattered, as they hop from one thing to another without ever settling down.

The Venusian number 6 is the epitome of grace, love, and beauty. It often aligns with people who have a deep-rooted sense of responsibility towards others. These individuals are often found in nurturing roles, taking care of families, communities, or causes that need compassion and kindness. However, they can sometimes become too involved, losing themselves in their roles as caregivers. The nurturing number 6 also has a penchant for artistic endeavours. Be it music, painting, or any form of art, people influenced by this number often find solace in artistic expression. But this focus on harmony and beauty can sometimes lead them to avoid confrontations and uncomfortable truths, both about themselves and the world around them.

The mystical number 7, under Neptune's influence, is an invitation to delve deeper into the unseen, the mysterious, and the spiritual. People influenced by this number often have an uncanny ability to understand the metaphysical aspects of existence. They are introspective, always pondering life's big questions, but this can sometimes make them distant or overly analytical. For number 7, the spiritual journey often includes a thirst for knowledge. They are always on the lookout for wisdom, often becoming lifelong students of various disciplines that interest them. However, this introspective lifestyle can sometimes make them aloof and disconnected from the practicalities of everyday life.

The Saturn-governed number 8 signifies authority and material success. It brings with it a kind of managerial efficiency, making people excellent in business and other pursuits that require strategic thinking. However, it can also engender a kind of tunnel vision where the goal becomes more important than the journey, often leading to workaholic tendencies. The ambitious number 8 also symbolizes an incredible resilience. These individuals can bounce back from setbacks like no other. They have an innate understanding of the ebb and flow of opportunities. However, this intense focus on success can sometimes make them appear materialistic or too engrossed in worldly affairs.

Lastly, the Mars-influenced number 9 represents the warrior spirit, but also a kind of global consciousness. People associated with this number often have a broad view of life, looking at issues from a humanitarian perspective. They have a fiery, assertive nature that propels them to action. However, they can sometimes become too impassioned, forgetting to take into account the nuances of a situation. The humanitarian tendencies of number 9 also encompass a rich emotional depth. These individuals are often highly empathetic, experiencing the feelings and moods of those around them. While this makes them excellent in social causes, it can also weigh heavily on them emotionally, leading to burnout or emotional exhaustion.

Master Numbers

In the realm of Chaldean numerology, Master Numbers are seen as unique and influential. These aren't just any numbers; we're talking about 11, 22, and 33. These Master Numbers are considered powerful and are not reduced to single-digit forms. Each of them has its own characteristics and implications that extend beyond the scope of the usual single-digit numbers. While the numbers 11, 22, and 33 are often discussed, some numerologists even extend the concept to include numbers like 44, 55, and so on. However, the first three remain the most commonly recognized and discussed.

Starting with 11, this number is often linked with intuition, spiritual insight, and enlightenment and is often seen as the 'Intuitive Illuminator'. It's as if the person with this number has an antenna tuned to a different frequency. This is a number that calls you towards intuition and insight. They're deeply perceptive, have an uncanny sense of the world's undercurrents, and often show a clear knack for recognizing patterns that most people overlook. But this heightened sensitivity isn't without its downsides. If you're an 11, you may find yourself easily overwhelmed, emotionally or mentally, by the very insights that make you special. It's crucial for you to create an environment that allows you to ground yourself, to not get lost in the maze of your intuitive capabilities. An 11 can be seen as an instinctual being, someone who has a higher sense of perception and understanding. But to balance this, the 11 also has a great responsibility to apply this understanding in a constructive manner. A misused 11 can veer towards self-deception or the misuse of power. Thus, it's important for an 11 to ground themselves in reality and practicality.

On the other hand, the 22 is the 'Master Builder', and this is a calling towards great achievement and is all about turning dreams into reality. If 11 is the dreamer, then 22 is the doer. People with this number often become leaders in their fields, not by accident, but through a systematic, well-thought-out approach to career and life planning. People with this number possess the visionary qualities of the 11 but pair it with a grounded, practical ability to achieve their goals. These are the people you want in charge of projects, the ones who can see both the forest and the trees. However, it's not a free ride; the pressure to achieve can be crushing, and a 22 has to be careful of becoming too materialistic or overly focused on their goals, to the point where they lose sight of what's really important. The universe has given them a higher calling, and they have to remember to use their powers for the greater good. Those with this Master Number need to learn how to manage their stress levels, as the high expectations they set for themselves can lead to burnout if they're not careful.

Lastly, we have the number 33, the 'Master Teacher', is often engaged in some form of healing or nurturing, whether physical or spiritual, imbued with compassion and a deep understanding of human nature. People with this Master Number often find themselves in roles where they can mentor, guide, and heal others. They are naturally inclined to fields like education, healthcare, and social work. The nature of this number is so giving and loving that the challenge often becomes about setting boundaries. The willingness to help and guide others is admirable but can turn into a drawback if you forget to take care of yourself in the process. People with this number can become the rock in a community, the person everyone turns to for wisdom and guidance. While this is rewarding, it can also be draining. A 33 must take time out to nurture themselves, replenish their own energy stores, so they can continue to serve others.

Master Numbers are like double-edged swords. They provide people with incredible talents and potential for success but come with their own sets of unique challenges. Being aware of these Master Numbers in your numerological profile can give you a more nuanced understanding of your abilities and the hurdles you may face. But remember, these numbers don't dictate your fate; they merely offer you a broader palette of options and challenges. How you use this knowledge is, as always, entirely up to you. And so, with these Master Numbers, it's as if the universe is handing you a set of powerful tools, but also asking for something in return. These tools come with lessons that often require you to take on added responsibilities. In essence, these Master Numbers are not just indicators of potential but also markers of the higher expectations that you should have of yourself.

They serve as both a map and a warning sign, pointing out the easier routes you can take but also alerting you to the bumps and turns ahead. And while these numbers offer no guarantees of a smooth journey, they do promise that the trip will be enriching, allowing you to learn important lessons and, if you're willing, to become a more thoughtful and insightful person along the way. So if you find one of these Master Numbers in your chart, recognize its potency. Make a conscious effort to steer this potent energy in a constructive direction. In the end, understanding the powerful nature of these Master Numbers is like being handed a key to a hidden room. It's up to you to unlock the door and explore the vastness that lies beyond.

Other Double Digits Number

Unlike Pythagorean numerology, Chaldeans researched and had drawn a detailed picture of double digits also. Apart from Master numbers as discussed, they have given us the properties and nature of each of the other numbers. They have some pretty straight forward numbers, some cautionary numbers, some pretty complex numbers like 13. But as we said earlier, it's a much bigger and complex subject which could not be covered in the scope of this book. I will try to give a glimpse of what the number 13 meant to the Chaldeans as an example. In Chaldean numerology, the number 13 stands as a symbol of disruption and transformation. It's akin to a catalyst that shakes up the existing order. The idea of 13 being an unlucky or fearsome number likely takes roots from Christian beliefs, where it's often associated with irregularity and imbalance, notably in scenarios like the Last Supper with Jesus and his 12 apostles, making him the 13th figure.

When you come across this number, it's almost like a cosmic nudge to question the status quo. The 13 doesn't tread lightly; it comes to topple, rebuild, or instigate revolutionary changes. It's the number that challenges existing norms and forces individuals or systems to re-evaluate their foundations. However, it's essential to understand that the number 13 isn't innately good or bad; it's a force of change. Whether the outcome of this change results in positive or negative consequences is often determined by a myriad of other factors such as timing, individual personalities, and the larger context in which this change occurs. It's not the harbinger of doom but rather a call to action, compelling us to rethink, rebuild, and evolve.

Today, Chaldean Numerology is not merely a historical artifact but an evolving field of study. Its tenets have survived the test of time, and its applicability spans multiple domains—from personal development to interpersonal relationships to even career choices. Its versatility makes it universally appealing, and its resilience ensures its continued relevance. The beauty of Chaldean Numerology lies in its adaptability and the depth of its scope. It stands as a testament to human curiosity and the perpetual quest for understanding the unknown. As a discipline, it invites us all to delve deeper into the complex interplay of numbers and human experience, urging us to explore beyond the visible and question beyond the obvious. In doing so, Chaldean Numerology offers a profound, enriching lens through which to view ourselves and the universe we inhabit.

Chapter Thirteen

Vedic Numerology

The root of Indian systems of Numerology

In the world of numerology, Indian Numerology holds a unique place, striking a delicate balance between ancient mysticism and tangible self-improvement. Anchored in the cultural backdrop of Indian mythology, this system transcends the realm of pseudoscience through its multifaceted approach, potential for self-realization, and steadfast ethical foundation.

Indian Numerology taps into the country's rich philosophical backdrop, viewing numbers as not just digits but carriers of cosmic energy. It offers insights into a person's place in the universe by decoding numbers tied to their name and birthdate. Various systems like Vedic, Tamil, Buddhist, and Jainist numerology offer distinct approaches, but Vedic Numerology serves as the foundational structure.

In Vedic Numerology, numbers are intertwined with astrology, and Sanskrit letters are assigned numerical values. This system aims to reveal deep insights into an individual's motivations and life paths through concepts like Soul Urge Numbers and Destiny Numbers. Tamil Numerology, mainly practiced in Tamil Nadu, focuses on planetary influences and uses Tamil letters for its numerical values. It helps to unveil an individual's character traits and possible life journey through Birth, Destiny, and Name Numbers. Buddhist Numerology uses numbers as spiritual tools; for example, the sacred number 108 is considered cosmic. Numbers are used to enhance meditation and spiritual practices. Jainist Numerology, meanwhile, has its roots in Jainism and links numbers to virtues and spiritual growth, guiding practitioners on their spiritual journey.

While these numerology systems differ in practices and interpretations, they share a common thread. At their core, they recognize the profound connection between numbers, cosmic energies, and human experiences. Vedic Numerology serves as the base that unites these diverse approaches, providing a foundational understanding of the intricate relationship between numbers and spirituality. Amidst the diversity, Indian Numerology reflects the pluralistic ethos of India itself. Practitioners and seekers find resonance in different systems based on their cultural backgrounds and spiritual beliefs. This multiplicity allows individuals to explore various dimensions of their personalities, destinies, and cosmic connections. Whether rooted in Vedic, Tamil, Buddhist, or Jainist numerology, the pursuit of self-discovery and alignment with universal energies remains a common goal, uniting these various branches of Indian Numerology. In this context, we will delve deeper into the intricacies of the Vedic Numerology system.

Vedic Numerology

Vedic Numerology finds its roots entwined with the rich narratives of Indian mythology. However, it rises above mere esotericism by offering a structured framework that amalgamates time-honoured wisdom with numerical calculations. This harmonious fusion allows for a distinctive approach that unites spiritual insights with pragmatic applications, setting it apart from the realm of pseudoscience. The methodology of Vedic Numerology showcases a remarkable adaptability by assigning numbers to sounds, and this is facilitated by the structure of Sanskrit, an ancient and highly phonetic language. This approach enables Vedic Numerology to transcend linguistic boundaries and be applied effectively to various languages, offering a versatile system for self-discovery and insight across cultures. Sanskrit, known for its precise phonetic system, has a unique attribute: each of its letters corresponds to a specific sound. This comprehensive set of phonetic representations in Sanskrit forms the basis for assigning numbers to sounds. As a result, Vedic Numerology manages to integrate both sounds and letters into its methodology, allowing it to be applied universally.

In this methodology, the focus shifts from the alphabetic representation of words to the phonetic representation of sounds. Each sound produced in speech is associated with a particular numerical value. The belief underlying this methodology is that every sound carries a distinct vibrational frequency that aligns with specific numerical attributes, in line with numerology's core concept. For example, consider the Sanskrit word "shanti", which translates to "peace". Each phonetic element of this word – "sha", "a", "na", "ti" – corresponds to specific numerical values based on Sanskrit's phonetic structure. These values are then summed and reduced to a single digit, revealing the numerological interpretation of the word.

The brilliance of this approach is enhanced by Sanskrit's phonetic intricacy, which provides a sound-letter pairing for every phoneme. This comprehensive phonetic system ensures that no sound is left unrepresented, enabling the assignment of numbers to sounds with precision. Consequently, the methodology becomes applicable to any language that can be phonetically translated, whether it's English, Mandarin, Arabic, or others. By integrating Sanskrit's phonetic structure, Vedic Numerology bridges the gap between diverse languages and cultures. The underlying principle acknowledges the fundamental nature of human expression and communication through sounds. This recognition ensures that the system is not confined by linguistic differences, thereby offering individuals from various linguistic backgrounds an opportunity to explore the insights and wisdom that Vedic Numerology provides.

Vedic Numerology and its philosophy

Vedic Numerology, an ancient practice steeped in Indian tradition, offers more than just a fascinating exploration of the mystical; it provides a detailed roadmap to understanding human nature and the world around us. The planets play pivotal roles here. Consider Jupiter, the planet associated with wisdom, growth, and benevolence. When you look at individuals influenced by Jupiter, you'll notice these characteristics are often vividly imprinted on their personalities. Similarly, Venus, the planet often surrounded by an aura of love and beauty, imparts these very traits on the people it governs. This isn't a game of mere chance; it's deeply rooted in the rich tapestry of Indian spirituality.

These associations go beyond Indian culture and tap into universal archetypes. These are patterns of behaviour and emotion that are found across cultures and serve as common denominators in the human experience. Essentially, the system speaks a global language, making Vedic Numerology a universal tool for understanding the core of human nature. But the brilliance of Vedic Numerology doesn't end with individual analysis; it expands into the practical realm of life. It serves as an excellent guide for self-improvement, steering people toward understanding their strengths and weaknesses. This aspect harmonizes well with the tenets of modern psychology, providing a complementary perspective that enriches our understanding of ourselves and those around us.

Adding a layer of ethical depth to the system, Vedic Numerology insists on a responsible use of this ancient wisdom. The focus is not on exploiting the knowledge for short-term gains, but rather on channelling it for personal and societal improvement. The system continually emphasizes the importance of integrity and ethical understanding, which in turn strengthens its credibility and reliability. Vedic Numerology is not merely a subject of curiosity or mystical pondering. It is a nuanced and comprehensive system that bridges the wisdom of ancient India with the challenges and complexities of modern life. Through its detailed analysis and ethical guidelines, Vedic Numerology serves as a lighthouse, guiding us through the complicated terrain of human emotions, motivations, and relationships, all while illuminating our path toward a richer, more fulfilled life. It's a remarkable field that brings the cosmic dance down to earth, helping us navigate the complexities of our human journey with a little more wisdom and a lot more insight.

Vedic Numerology, often met with a mix of fascination and scepticism, has an uncanny way of speaking to the depths of the human soul by interlinking celestial symbols with earthly personality traits. The blending of these cosmic elements with human attributes creates an intriguing tapestry that many find too mystical to be scientific, leading to debates and discussions among scholars who worry about the potential for pseudoscience. Yet, what often gets missed in this chorus of scepticism is the transformative potential Vedic Numerology offers not just for personal development, but for understanding complex human behaviours and even improving leadership qualities across various sectors of society.

When we consider the role of Vedic Numerology at the individual level, we find that it serves as an intriguing reflective mirror that offers deep insights into the inner workings of our minds and souls. This is not just a simple inventory of characteristics, but a complex guide that opens doors to self-awareness and offers pathways to personal growth and psychological well-being. The real beauty of Vedic Numerology lies in its universal applicability, as it transcends cultural and social boundaries by tapping into archetypal symbols and numbers that have global resonance. This makes it a potent tool that can foster better understanding and harmony in multicultural societies.

Now let's turn our gaze to a broader canvas: the application of Vedic Numerology in the realm of leadership and community building. Leaders who can navigate the intricacies of this ancient system will find themselves armed with a rich repertoire of insights that can inform and guide their leadership styles in ways that are deeply connected with the needs and aspirations of the people they lead. The potential here is immense; by tuning into the unique vibrational frequencies that each number symbolizes; leaders can cultivate teams where every member feels genuinely understood and valued. This is transformative leadership at its best, where the leader becomes a facilitator of not just productivity but also human flourishing.

While the mystical overtones of Vedic Numerology may continue to be a subject of debate, it is unwise to overlook the profound practical wisdom embedded within it. We live in a world where the quest for self-awareness and effective leadership is more important than ever, and Vedic Numerology offers us valuable tools to meet these challenges. So, let us keep our minds open to the possibilities that this ancient wisdom offers us, and who knows, we might just find the keys to unlocking the best versions of ourselves and our communities.

Vedic Numerology and Indian Astrology

At their core, Vedic Numerology and Indian astrology share a cultural heritage deeply embedded in Vedic and Hindu traditions. Emerging from the same source, they reflect the rich interplay between cosmic energies and the human journey. In Vedic Numerology, numbers take centre stage as carriers of profound meaning and vibrations. The practice involves assigning significance to these numbers, thereby shaping an individual's life path and destiny. Meanwhile, Indian astrology draws insights from planetary positions and celestial movements, deciphering their impact on life's myriad facets.

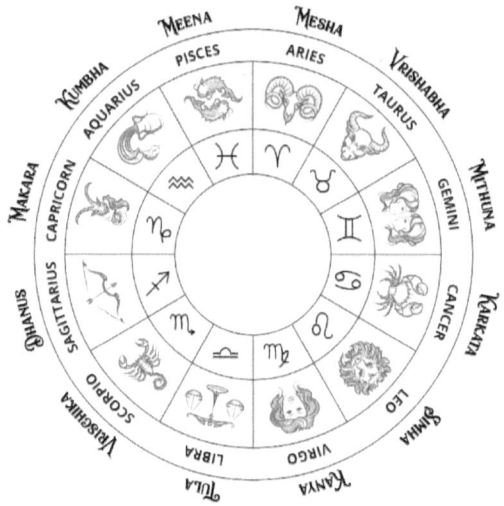

Rashi Chakra or the Zodiac Wheel

Both systems delve into an individual's life journey, offering insights that can illuminate the path ahead. Vedic Numerology deciphers auspicious dates, compatible partnerships, and suitable professions based on calculated numbers. In a parallel vein, Indian astrology guides seekers by providing insights into relationships, career choices, health concerns, and other life dimensions through planetary influences.

However, while there are threads of commonality, Vedic Numerology and Indian astrology diverge in several significant ways. Vedic Numerology revolves around numbers and their intricate meanings. It analyses birth dates and names, unveiling the core vibrations that shape an individual's personality, strengths, weaknesses, and life trajectory. In contrast, Indian astrology's foundation lies in the celestial map of one's birth, meticulously charting the positions of planets and their interplay across different houses. In the context of predictions, Indian astrology offers a comprehensive array of insights, including the impact of planetary transits and dasha periods, marking pivotal shifts or challenges in one's journey. Vedic Numerology, while insightful, does not provide the nuanced time-specific predictions that Indian astrology does.

Furthermore, the symbolism inherent in each system differs. Vedic Numerology attributes unique meanings to individual numbers and their combinations, forging a distinct language of interpretation. On the other hand, Indian astrology relies on the symbolic significance of planets, signs, houses, and aspects to unravel the complex spectrum of aspects of an individual's life. In the broader context, both Vedic Numerology and Indian astrology contribute to a holistic understanding of an individual's path. While numerology draws from numbers to shed light on destiny, astrology navigates the celestial landscape to offer guidance. These systems, rooted in ancient wisdom, guide individuals toward self-discovery, personal growth, and a deeper connection with the cosmic rhythms that shape their journey.

Vedic Numerology weaves cosmic energies and numbers together, shedding light on the intricate bonds between our lives and the universe. Through 81 possible combinations of psychic and destiny numbers, Vedic Numerology unveils life's mosaic. Amid the vast realm of Jyotish's possibilities, Vedic Numerology stands as a focused lens. Imagine selecting a vehicle guided by Vedic Numerology and your birth chart. The 4th House, representing vehicles, takes centre stage. The planets within it hold clues. Each planet carries a unique energy, and their placements matter. For instance, consider Cancer as the ruler of your 4th House, with Saturn's presence. Saturn aligns with number 8. Focus on the Moon, linked to the 4th House. Is it forming positive connections? Identify the stronger planet.

Decoding You

Saturn and the Moon contend. If Saturn prevails, number 8 holds sway. If the Moon takes the lead, it signifies number 2.

Houses also hold significance when selecting a house or apartment number. The 4th House's ruler shapes the narrative. In your birth chart, both psychic and destiny numbers matter. A destiny number of 9 connects to Mars, while a destiny number of 3 resonates with Jupiter. Vedic Numerology deciphers cosmic tales. Birth charts blend celestial stories with life's journey. Guided by Vedic Numerology, the interplay of numbers and planets crafts a unique melody for each individual, transcending time and space.

Chapter Fourteen

The Kaṭapayādi System

Encrypting knowledge of numbers inside letters

The repository of ancient wisdom accessible to us today flourished through an enduring oral tradition. From its origins in Vedic literature, upon which Indic thought is rooted, this oral tradition's roots run deep and wide. Even when knowledge was transcribed, it often assumed terse forms, leaving space for commentaries and explanations. Bhashyas, explanatory notes, became an integral facet of the Indic tradition.

Contrary to the misconception that this oral tradition was exclusive, it was all-encompassing. Ancient Indian educational systems welcomed learners irrespective of social standing, and knowledge was openly shared. The emphasis, however, lay in preserving the purity of sound as sound imparts meaning to words. Pronunciation and accurate memorization were held in high regard to ensure the true essence of information. This was particularly relevant for Sanskrit and Indic languages, where the auditory aspects of words (dhwani) are tightly interwoven with their meanings. This approach to preserving and transmitting knowledge through speech led to the development of two main systems – Akshara Samkhya and Bhuta Samkhya. In the Akshara Samkhya system, numbers were mapped to Sanskrit alphabet letters, while the Bhuta Samkhya system associated numbers with objects or specific words. In this discussion, we delve into the Akshara Samkhya system, popularly known as Kaṭapayādi.

The Kaṭapayādi system, also known as the Akshara Samkhya system, involves encoding numbers into Sanskrit alphabets. This seemingly cryptographic technique wasn't designed to conceal knowledge; instead, it facilitated the memorization of unique numbers, mathematical values, formulae, constants, event dates, and more. By embedding these numbers into prose or poetry, this method provided a convenient memory aid. The system's rules are straightforward, allowing for easy decoding.

The origin of the Kaṭapayādi system remains shrouded in mystery, with Vararuchi, a renowned scholar from Kerala in the fourth century CE, often attributed to it. His work "Chandra-Vakhyas", a collection of Sanskrit sentences for lunar position calculations, contains one of the earliest documented instances of the Kaṭapayādi scheme. This connection suggests Vararuchi's potential role as the system's creator. Although debates persist regarding the dating of "Chandra-Vakhyas", subsequent scholars such as Aryabhata I (5th century CE) and Haridatta (7th century CE) demonstrated familiarity with the Kaṭapayādi scheme. This scheme also found application in the works of scholars from the Madhava to Sankara Varman lineage, spanning the 14th to 18th centuries CE in Kerala. Their contributions in written form provide tangible evidence of Kaṭapayādi extensive usage in Kerala.

Kaṭapayādi's presence extends to the Malayalam language, where it is referred to as "Paral Peru". The Malayalam term "paral" means the shells of miniature shellfish. The practice of employing miniature seashells as counting frames in Kerala's predictive astrology underscores this connection. Presently, astrological calculations involve recalling verses with numerical meanings encoded using Kaṭapayādi. This interplay likely contributed to the local term "paral-peru" for Kaṭapayādi in Kerala.

Kaṭapayādi's significance is underscored by its endurance across oral and written traditions in Vedic Numerology. This system's essence lies in assigning numbers to Sanskrit letters, and given that Sanskrit is a phonetically based language, the numbers are inherently linked to sounds rather than just letters. As a result, translating the assigned numbers into Latin/Roman-based alphabet equivalents might not be wholly accurate. This nuanced interplay between sounds and numbers makes Kaṭapayādi a distinctive and intriguing method within the realm of Vedic Numerology.

Group	1	2	3	4	5	6	7	8	9	0
Ka - varg	क ka	ख kha	ग ga	घ gha	ङ nga	च cha	छ chha	ज ja	झ jha	ञ nja/nya
Ta - varg	ट ṭa	ठ ṭha	ड ḍa	ढ ḍha	ण ṇa	त ta	थ tha	द da	ध dha	न na
Pa - varg	प pa	फ pha	ब ba	भ bha	म ma	-	-	-	-	-
Ya - varg	य ya	र ra	ल la	व va	श śa	ष sha	स sa	ह ha	-	-

The Kaṭapayādi system employs a distinctive classification method for Sanskrit letters that differs from the conventional division into guttural, palatal, cerebral, dental, and labial vargas. Instead, Kaṭapayādi groups the Sanskrit consonants into distinct groups based on the initial sounds of certain groups of letters. These groups are often referred to as the "ka-group", "ta-group", "pa-group", and "ya-group".

The vowels in the Kaṭapayādi system are generally assigned the numerical value of zero. In case of a conjunct, consonants attached to a non-vowel will be valueless. For example, *kya* (क्य) is formed by, *k* (क्) + *y* (य्) + *a* (अ). The only consonant standing with a vowel is *ya* (य). So, the corresponding numeral

Decoding You

for *kya* (क्य) will be 1. Indians used the Hindu–Arabic numeral system for numbering, traditionally written in increasing place values from left to right. This is as per the rule "अङ्कानां वामतो गतिः" which means numbers go from right to left

By classifying Sanskrit letters into these distinct groups based on their initial sounds, the Kaṭapayādi system enables the association of specific numerical values with each group. The mapping of numbers to these groups forms the foundation of the Kaṭapayādi system's encoding method. This system of classification is unique to the Kaṭapayādi system and serves as a fundamental framework for encoding numerical values within Sanskrit texts and verses. It reflects the intricate relationship between the phonetic qualities of Sanskrit letters and the numerical values they represent, offering a distinct perspective within the realm of Vedic Numerology.

For example, the book "Karana Paddhati" of 15th century has a sloka encoded in Kaṭapayādi which gives us the value of *'pi'*

anūnanūnnānananunnanityai
ssmāhatāścakra kalāvibhaktoḥ
caṇḍāṃśucandrādhamakuṃbhipālair
vyāsastadarddhaṃ tribhamaurvika syāt

It gives the circumference of a circle of diameter, *anūnanūnnānananunnanityai* which is (10,000,000,000) as *caṇḍāṃśucandrādhamakuṃbhipālair* means (31415926536).

***

Chapter Fifteen

System of Vedic Numerology

The aspects and methodologies

Within the realm of Vedic Numerology, a vast array of numbers takes centre stage, each bearing its own distinct essence and relevance. These numbers form the backbone of this ancient system, illuminating various facets of an individual's existence, character, and destiny. As we journey through the labyrinth of these numbers, we uncover their significance and how they interweave with our lives.

There are three primary numbers associated with an individual in Vedic numerology:

1. Psychic Number
2. Destiny Number
3. Name Number.

The Psychic Number represents an individual's nature and character and is calculated using the day of birth. The Destiny Number represents an individual's destiny and how others perceive them and is calculated using the entire date of birth. The Name Number is calculated using an individual's name and represents the vibrations and energy associated with their name.

Decoding You

These numbers can provide insight into an individual's personality, strengths, weaknesses, and potential. They can also be used to make predictions about an individual's future and to guide them towards a fulfilling life. In this chapter, we will explore these numbers in detail and learn how to calculate and interpret them. These numbers, like intricate brushstrokes on the canvas of life, contribute to the rich treasure of Vedic Numerology. As we unravel their meanings, we gain profound insights into the layers of our existence, embracing a holistic understanding of the dynamic interplay between numbers and human experiences.

The Psychic Number

The Psychic Number, in the intriguing dance of Vedic Numerology, emerges as a cornerstone that helps us understand who we truly are from our very first steps in this world. It's a numerical essence that comes to us when we're born and stays with us, shaping our worldview and personal characteristics, until about 35 years of age. The core idea here is straightforward: this number is derived simply from your birth date.

For instance, if someone was born on the 23rd of the month, the calculation would be 2 + 3 = 5, resulting in a Psychic Number of 5.

So, why is this number so important? The Psychic Number acts like a guidepost, orienting us in the myriad complexities of life. From our childhood years filled with curiosity to the adult phase where we start to make sense of the world, this number acts as a constant backdrop. It's not just a number but a lens, a perspective that colours everything we see, feel, and experience. Those initial 35 years of life, which for many of us are full of trials, tribulations, and self-discovery, are particularly influenced by the Psychic Number. During this span, the number serves as an anchor, offering insights into what makes us tick and how we interact with the world around us.

The richness of this concept becomes even more interesting when we consider how the Psychic Number interacts with another crucial element in Vedic Numerology: the Destiny Number. It's like a cosmic duet. While the

Psychic Number encapsulates our inherent traits, the Destiny Number talks about our life's purpose and the fate that awaits us. The balance between these two numbers becomes a kind of lifelong quest. If you can harmonize an odd Psychic Number, which is said to have masculine and dynamic energy, with an even Destiny Number, representing feminine and static qualities, you've got the best of both worlds. This balance enriches our experiences and adds depth to our understanding of ourselves and our paths in life.

All in all, the Psychic Number serves as more than just a numeral value. It's a close companion on our journey through life, particularly in those formative years where we're still trying to figure out who we are and what we're supposed to do. The number doesn't just quantify; it qualifies, adding texture to our understanding of ourselves and the worlds we inhabit. So, the next time you delve into the realm of Vedic Numerology, pay close attention to your Psychic Number. It might just hold the keys to understanding the deep recesses of your personality and guiding you through the maze that is life.

Destiny Number

The Destiny Number is an intriguing element in Vedic Numerology, especially for those who've crossed the age of 35. This is the time when you may start asking deeper questions about where your life is heading and what legacy you'll leave behind. At this stage, the Destiny Number becomes your guiding light. Unlike the Psychic Number, which is more about your natural tendencies and shapes your personality in the early years, the Destiny Number represents your life's journey as a whole. It talks about your ambitions, talents, and the challenges and opportunities that will come your way.

Calculating this number isn't rocket science. You add up all the digits of your complete birth date until you're left with a single-digit number. Say, for instance, your birth date is 15th March 1982. You add all those numbers up—1, 5, 3, 1, 9, 8, 2—and get 29. Now, 2 plus 9 equals 11, and further reducing it, 1 plus 1 is 2. That's your Destiny Number. This number is like a well-placed signboard on a highway, directing you towards the path you're meant

Decoding You

to take. It provides pointers on what sort of jobs you'll excel at, what kind of challenges you'll face, and how best you can fulfil your deeper life goals.

Here's the interesting part: the Destiny Number doesn't work in isolation. As mentioned, it operates in tandem with your Psychic Number. While the Psychic Number lays the foundation in the early stages of your life, helping you navigate your likes, dislikes, and immediate reactions to situations, the Destiny Number comes into play later. Think of it as a secondary layer of paint on a well-primed canvas. The Destiny Number fills in the details, accentuating the traits you've always had, adding depth to your character, and making you more self-aware. It's as if the Psychic Number sets up the basic plot of your life story, and the Destiny Number adds the twists, conflicts, and resolutions that make the narrative complete and uniquely yours.

Name Number

The Name Number in numerology is pretty important when it comes to understanding yourself. It's one of four main numbers that tell you about different parts of your life. Now, the Name Number is a real gem when you want to know how you come across in your job and among your friends. In fact, if you're wondering about your career or how you fit into a team, this is the number to look at. This whole idea comes from ancient teachings that say numbers can reveal a lot about you. Especially in the Vedic tradition, numbers are considered really powerful in understanding your personality and even predicting big moments in your life. So, your Name Number isn't just a random digit; it's like a tool that helps you understand your social and work life better.

Let's get this straight in simple terms. Your Name Number is a big deal because it's like a mirror to your personality and even your destiny. This idea isn't new; it goes back to ancient times when people believed that each letter in your name has a special energy, a kind of vibe. When you add up these vibes, you get your Name Number. And this number is thought to connect you to the bigger picture, the energy of the universe itself. The way this number vibrates can either pull good experiences towards you or push them away. So, when you know your Name Number, you get a sense of how you fit into the world and what kind of energy you're likely to attract or repel.

The interpretations of numbers are intricately tied to their connections with celestial bodies and the empirical observations of their influence on human lives over countless years. Whether exploring Vedic name numerology or engaging with Western systems of number interpretation, the undeniable potency of numbers remains consistent. Modern science even acknowledges that life itself can be deconstructed into a series of binary elements, while the intricate fabric of the universe can be deciphered through the lens of numerological equations.

Amidst this profound exploration, it's essential to exercise discernment. Embracing both the mystic and the scientist within, practitioners of name numerology should approach their interpretations with a balanced perspective. The enchantment inherent in numbers should be harmonized with pragmatic sensibility, ensuring that insights gained are insightful and accurate. As the mystique of numbers intertwines with the rationality of interpretation, a comprehensive understanding of our inner selves unfolds, guided by the wisdom encoded in names.

The flexibility of our name number is a distinctive trait in Vedic astrology, as it can be altered by changing the name itself. This allows individuals to consciously select which aspects of their personality they wish to exhibit to others. The choice of which name to analyse numerologically becomes relevant due to the various names we are addressed by in different contexts. This is a result of the diverse qualities we demonstrate in interactions with different groups of people.

Our behaviour can significantly differ in various settings. The relaxed demeanour at home is in contrast to the focused attitude at work or the unguarded manner around acquaintances. This inherent flexibility grants us the capacity to choose which facets of our personality to showcase. Each of our names harbours a distinct numerological code that unveils a specific facet of ourselves to those addressing us by that name.

The first name uncovers insights into an individual's character, inherent talents, temperament, and energy. This analysis reveals the planetary influence that shapes an individual's energy, talents, and individuality. The middle name discloses essential potential and the fusion of education and personal characteristics. It provides a glimpse into the planet governing one's fundamental potential and distinctive qualities. From a karmic standpoint, the last name holds significance. It unravels hereditary traits and talents transmitted across generations and offers insight into the planetary influence on ancestral karma and karmic lessons for the family.

The composite analysis of the full name yields the most vital and substantial name number in numerology. It's important to recognize that the name number can vary in different situations, resulting in diverse perceptions of an individual. Additionally, factors such as marriage, leading to a change in the last name, can reshape life and karma, often inducing unforeseen changes. In numerology analysis, individuals often consider their "public names" – typically the combination of the first and last names. Notably, the first letter of the public name exerts a profound influence on an individual.

The process of calculating the Name Number primarily follows a phonetic approach, harmonizing with the phonetic structure of the Sanskrit language. This practice not only echoes the ancient Sanskrit-based numerology but also resonates with the vibrational nature of the language itself.

In the ever-evolving modern era, a notable shift has surfaced. The practice of assigning numerical values to English alphabets of a name has gained prominence in calculating the Name Number. It is crucial to recognize that this method aligns more with Chaldean Numerology rather than the authentic Vedic Numerology. The essence of embracing the phonetic approach, embodied by Kaṭapayādi, lies in its seamless integration with the Sanskrit language—a feature deeply interwoven with Vedic philosophy and culture. Utilizing the Roman alphabet to ascertain numerical values is not inherently erroneous; however, it may not seamlessly mesh with the predictive framework of Vedic Numerology, which is firmly rooted in the ancient wisdom of the Sanskrit-based phonetic system.

Calculating Name Number

Let's consider the name Arya Sharma (/'aːrjə 'ʃərmaː/). Using the Kaṭapayādi system, we assign numerical values to each consonant as follows – and notice that we are not assigning numbers to the Roman alphabets of the name, but the numbers are assigned phonetically.

Name: अर्य शर्मा (Arya Sharma)

अ	र	य	श	र	म
A	R	Y	Sh	R	M
0	2	1	3	2	4

Now, let's calculate the Name Number by summing up the numerical values of each consonant: $0 + 2 + 1 + 3 + 2 + 4 = 12$

Since the total is 12, we further reduce it to a single digit by adding the digits together: $1 + 2 = 3$

Therefore, the Name Number for "Arya Sharma" using the Kaṭapayādi system is 3.

Please note that this calculation uses the Kaṭapayādi numerical values assigned to Sanskrit letters, which are not equivalent to standard numerical digits of the alphabets. The Kaṭapayādi system assigns numerical values to letters based on their phonetic similarity to Sanskrit letters, not the actual letters in English names. We have to write letters phonetically to obtain accurate results.

***

Chapter Sixteen

The Planets & Numbers

The Inextricable Relation with Numbers and Planets

The inter-relationship of the ruling planets associated with the psychic number, destiny number, and name number creates a dynamic framework that shapes an individual's life journey and character. A harmonious alignment between these influences can lead to a more coherent and fulfilling life, while conflicting influences may introduce challenges that prompt growth and self-discovery. Understanding and harnessing these interconnections can provide valuable insights for individuals seeking self-awareness and a deeper understanding of their life's path.

The psychic number ruling planet reflects an individual's inherent traits, natural inclinations, and core personality. This planet governs how one perceives oneself and interacts with the immediate environment. When this planet aligns harmoniously with the ruling planets of the destiny and name numbers, it can create a sense of congruence between the individual's self-perception and their life's path. On the contrary, conflicting influences between these ruling planets may lead to inner conflicts and challenges in self-expression.

The destiny number ruling planet, on the other hand, offers insights into an individual's life purpose, goals, and overall direction. When the ruling planet of the destiny number is well-aligned with the other ruling planets, it can facilitate a smoother journey towards fulfilling one's aspirations. However, when there is discord between these influences, individuals may experience obstacles and difficulties in achieving their intended life path.

The name number ruling planet pertains to an individual's expression in the outer world, how they present themselves to others, and their interactions within society. The relationship between the ruling planet of the name number and the other ruling planets can impact how an individual's inner qualities are projected outwardly. A harmonious alignment may result in a congruent representation of one's character, while conflicting influences might lead to misunderstandings or challenges in communication.

The interplay of these ruling planets can also indicate areas of strength and potential challenges. For instance, if the ruling planet of the psychic number is well-aligned with the ruling planet of the destiny number, an individual might naturally excel in pursuing their life's purpose. Similarly, if the ruling planet of the name number resonates positively with the ruling planet of the destiny number, it could support effective communication of goals and intentions. Conversely, conflicting influences among these ruling planets may result in internal conflicts or external challenges. An individual might feel torn between their innate traits and their intended life path, leading to a sense of inner discord. Additionally, misalignment between the name number's ruling planet and the destiny number's ruling planet might hinder effective communication of goals and aspirations.

For example, the number 1 is connected to the Sun, representing qualities like leadership and confidence. The number 2 is tied to the Moon, symbolizing sensitivity and intuition. This connection goes beyond symbolism; it's thought that planetary vibrations shape a person's life journey and karmic path. By understanding these resonances, Vedic numerology aims to reveal insights and navigate life's challenges. This relationship isn't limited to astrology; it's deeply woven into cultural practices and spiritual beliefs. The intricate link between numbers and planets reflects the holistic perspective of Indian spirituality. The bond between numbers and planets in Vedic numerology highlights the profound connection between cosmic energies and human existence, shaping both practical and spiritual aspects of life.

Number 1 - Sun (Surya) - The Sun, a radiant celestial body, is often regarded as the soul of the universe in Vedic astrology. It signifies the essence of life and vitality, illuminating both the physical and metaphysical realms. The Sun represents self-expression, willpower, and the core essence of an individual's identity.

- *Nature*: King, masculine, royal, Individualistic, authoritative, self-confident, original, structured.
- *Characteristics*: Original, creative, magnetic, truthful, influential.
- *Strengths*: Leadership, intelligence, charisma, influence, power.
- *Weaknesses*: Pride, ruthlessness, dominance, egocentrism, stubbornness, power-hungry, political

Number 2 - Moon (Chandra) - The Moon, a gentle and nurturing luminary, symbolizes emotions, instincts, and the subconscious mind. It reflects the inner world of an individual, unveiling their emotional landscape and intuitive capabilities.

- *Nature*: Queen, royal, more feminine, sensitive, intuitive, empathetic, ever-changing.
- *Characteristics*: Nurturing, reflective, imaginative, artistic, diplomatic.
- *Strengths*: Empathy, clever, compassion, intuition, nurturing, creativity, supportive.
- *Weaknesses*: Moodiness, emotional sensitivity, indecisiveness.

Number 3 - Jupiter (Guru) - Jupiter, often referred to as the 'Great Benefic,' is associated with wisdom, expansion, and abundance. It represents higher learning, spirituality, and the search for truth.

- *Nature*: Wise, teacher, talkative, prime-minister, optimistic, philosophical, religious, spiritual.
- *Characteristics*: Generous, wise, ethical, philosophical, idealistic, giver, happy, independent.
- *Strengths*: Wisdom, knowledge, growth, spirituality, creativity.
- *Weaknesses*: Excessive idealism, self-righteousness, extravagance, critical, weakness for sex.

Decoding You

Number 4 - Rahu - Rahu, the North Node of the Moon, is a shadow planet associated with desires, obsessions, and unfulfilled cravings. It represents a longing for material gains and worldly achievements.
- *Nature*: Ambitious, unconventional, seeking, unpredictable.
- *Characteristics*: Restless, ambitious, unconventional, materialistic, non-conformist.
- *Strengths*: Innovation, ambition, drive, practical, discipline, secretive, out-of-the-box.
- *Weaknesses*: Impulsiveness, deception, restlessness, disrespectful, accident-prone.

Number 5 - Mercury (Budha) - Mercury, the planet of communication and intellect, embodies the realm of thought, expression, and learning. It governs communication skills, adaptability, and analytical abilities.
- *Nature*: Intelligent, analytical, adaptable, youthful, prince.
- *Characteristics*: Quick-witted, articulate, logical, curious, intelligent, entertaining.
- *Strengths*: Communication, adaptability, versatility, business-acumen.
- *Weaknesses*: Overthinking, restlessness, superficiality, weak at relations, lack of concentration.

Number 6 - Venus (Shukra) - Venus, the planet of love and beauty, governs relationships, aesthetics, and sensual pleasures. It represents harmony, romance, and creativity.
- *Nature*: Charming, artistic, harmonious, pleasing, sensual.
- *Characteristics*: Romantic, diplomatic, sensual, artistic, slow yet thorough.
- *Strengths*: Harmony, aesthetic sense, charm, romanticism, luxury, beauty.
- *Weaknesses*: Indulgence, superficiality, vanity, lacks discipline, problem to say 'no'.

Number 7 – Ketu - Ketu, the South Node of the Moon, is a mysterious planet associated with spirituality, detachment, and past-life influences. It represents a release from material attachments and a search for enlightenment.

- *Nature*: Spiritual, introspective, detached, directionless, artistic, questioning.
- *Characteristics*: Spiritual, mystical, detached, introspective, philosophical, creative.
- *Strengths*: Depth, intuition, non-attachment, occult, suspicious nature, inventive.
- *Weaknesses*: Eccentricity, confusion, escapism, obsessiveness.

Number 8 - Saturn (Shani) - Saturn, known as the 'Great Malefic,' symbolizes responsibility, discipline, and challenges. It teaches valuable life lessons and represents the karmic influence in one's life.

- *Nature*: King-maker, disciplined, patient, practical.
- *Characteristics*: Enduring, responsible, disciplined, servant mentality.
- *Strengths*: Patience, perseverance, practicality, justice-seeking, occult, mysticism, judgement.
- *Weaknesses*: Pessimism, rigidity, fear of change, slow, depressive.

Number 9 - Mars (Mangal) - Mars, a fiery and dynamic planet, represents energy, ambition, and action. It is associated with passion, courage, and the drive to overcome challenges and obstacles.

- *Nature*: Energetic, masculine, ambitious, assertive, warrior, idealist, direct in talk.
- *Characteristics*: Courageous, determined, adventurous.
- *Strengths*: Determination, assertiveness, courage, action, no-nonsense, auspicious, leadership.
- *Weaknesses*: Impulsiveness, aggression, impatience.

These planetary influences play a significant role in shaping an individual's personality, strengths, weaknesses, and life experiences, based on their ruling number and astrological placements. The intricate interplay of these planetary energies gives rise to the complexity and uniqueness of each person's character.

The inter-relationship between planets

In Vedic numerology, the inter-relationship between planets holds a significant role, characterized by their status as friends, enemies, or neutrals. This classification shapes the dynamics of numerology by infusing planetary energies into our lives. Understanding these relationships sheds light on the intricate interplay of cosmic forces and their impact on our personalities and experiences.

Planets are categorized as friends when their energies align harmoniously. This alignment enhances the positive qualities associated with both planets, offering support and amplifying their combined influences. On the other hand, planets classified as enemies can create conflicting energies, leading to challenges and struggles in certain aspects of life. Neutral planets neither support nor oppose each other, fostering a neutral coexistence. While they don't actively enhance or diminish each other's influences, their presence in a numerological profile adds depth and complexity to the overall picture.

The interrelationship between planets serves as a guiding framework in numerology. Friendships and enmities between planets create a web of energies that influence our strengths, weaknesses, and life paths. This system underscores the importance of balance and synergy within our numerological makeup. The harmonious coexistence of planets as friends encourages the integration of diverse qualities, while the awareness of enemy planets prepares us to navigate challenges with resilience. Ultimately, the interplay between planets reflects the intricate dance of cosmic energies that shape our lives.

Sun: The Sun has Moon, Mars, and Jupiter as friends, is neutral towards Mercury, Venus, and Saturn, and considers Rahu (North Node) and Ketu (South Node) as enemies.

Moon: The Moon is friendly with Mercury, Venus, and Saturn. It is neutral towards Sun, Mars, and Jupiter, and doesn't have any enemies.

Mars: Mars has Jupiter and Moon as friends, is neutral towards Sun, Mercury, and Ketu, and considers Venus, Saturn, and Rahu as enemies.

Mercury: Mercury is friendly with Venus and Saturn, neutral towards Sun, Moon, and Mars, and is an enemy of Rahu and Ketu.

Jupiter: Jupiter has Mars and Moon as friends, is neutral towards Sun, Mercury, and Ketu, and is inimical with Venus, Saturn, and Rahu.

Venus: Venus is friendly with Mercury and Saturn, neutral towards Sun, Moon, and Ketu, and sees Mars, Jupiter, and Rahu as enemies.

Saturn: Saturn has Venus and Mercury as friends, is neutral towards Sun, Moon, and Ketu, and is an enemy of Mars, Jupiter, and Rahu.

Rahu (North Node): Rahu is friendly with Mercury, Venus, and Saturn. It is neutral towards Sun, Moon, and Mars, and considers Jupiter and Ketu as enemies.

Ketu (South Node): Ketu is friendly with Sun and Mars, is neutral towards Moon, Mercury, and Jupiter, and is an enemy of Venus, Saturn, and Rahu.

In the previous chapters, we got introduced to the concept of psychic numbers. Now, let's dive deeper by focusing on each psychic number from 1 to 9. Each of these numbers has its unique traits, shaping personalities, goals, and challenges. This chapter aims to give you a detailed look at what each number represents, helping you understand both yourself and those around you better. Get ready to explore these nine fascinating categories, where you'll learn how each number paints a distinct picture of human characteristics and potentials.

The Numbers

***The Psychic Number* 1** signifies individuals with innate leadership qualities, independence, and a pioneering spirit. These individuals are known for their originality, determination, and an unyielding drive to achieve their goals. Often seen as trailblazers, they initiate new ideas and ventures. At their core, Psychic Number 1 individuals possess an unwavering desire for leadership, drawing others to them through their magnetic presence. Their quest for independence fuels their actions, driving them to chart their own course regardless of conventional norms. This penchant for initiative positions them as pioneers, taking the first steps into uncharted territories. With determination as their ally, they move forward with unwavering resolve, even when faced with challenges. Their individuality shines through their unique perspective and creative thinking, setting them apart from the crowd.

Psychic Number 1 individuals' strengths lie in their unbreakable spirit and motivation. They excel at influencing and motivating others, making them effective leaders and initiators of change. Their clear vision and inspiring ideas pave the way for innovative approaches in various aspects of life. However, they may come across as overly assertive or dominant at times, and their insistence on independence might lead to challenges in collaboration or compromise. Impatience could be a stumbling block, particularly when immediate results aren't forthcoming. In careers, they thrive as entrepreneurs, innovators, CEOs, and leaders in diverse fields. Their charisma and visionary outlook attract opportunities aligned with making a significant impact.

In relationships, they seek partners who understand and respect their need for autonomy, thriving in partnerships that honour and nurture their independence. Their destiny centres on embracing their role as catalysts for change, shaping the world through their unique vision and inspiring others through their actions and unwavering self-belief. Psychic Number 1 individuals embody the archetype of visionary leaders and pioneers, leaving an indelible mark on society as change-makers and innovators.

***The Psychic Number* 2** is characterized by individuals who possess an innate sense of empathy, cooperation, and harmony. Like the gentle pull of the Moon's influence, they radiate a soothing aura that draws people towards them. Individuals with this number are known for their nurturing qualities, often playing the role of caregivers and supporters in various situations. Psychic Number 2 individuals are driven by a desire to create connections and foster unity, making them excellent mediators and peacemakers.

At their core, Psychic Number 2 individuals exude a natural empathy that enables them to understand and resonate with the emotions of others. This innate sensitivity allows them to offer a comforting presence, acting as a pillar of support for those around them. Their ability to cooperate and collaborate seamlessly stems from their belief in the power of unity and working together. This makes them adept at mediating conflicts and bringing people together to find common ground. Strengths of Psychic Number 2 individuals lie in their capacity to create warm, nurturing environments where people feel valued and understood. They excel at building strong relationships based on trust and mutual respect. Their intuition guides them in understanding the needs and emotions of others, allowing them to provide genuine assistance and support.

However, Psychic Number 2 individuals may sometimes struggle with setting healthy boundaries. Their selfless nature can lead them to prioritize others' needs above their own, potentially causing emotional strain. They may also experience moments of self-doubt, unsure of their own worth as they focus on caring for others.

In careers, Psychic Number 2 individuals thrive in roles that involve caregiving, counselling, teaching, and fields that require empathy and understanding. Their nurturing demeanour makes them excellent parents, mentors, therapists, and social workers. They possess the remarkable ability to create spaces where individuals feel safe and supported. In relationships, Psychic Number 2 individuals seek partners who appreciate and reciprocate their nurturing nature. They are drawn to those who understand the significance of emotional connections and value their efforts to create harmony. Their destiny centres around embracing their role as compassionate caregivers and bridge builders, using their empathetic nature to foster unity and understanding.

The Psychic Number 2 embodies the archetype of the nurturing caregiver and mediator. Their intuitive empathy and dedication to fostering connections empower them to leave a lasting impact on the lives they touch, making them invaluable contributors to a harmonious and compassionate world.

***The Psychic Number* 3** encapsulates individuals who radiate charisma, ambition, and a natural inclination towards achievement. Just as the number three signifies a harmonious trio, these individuals often excel in social settings, effortlessly captivating those around them. Psychic Number 3 is associated with qualities of confidence, adaptability, and a strong drive to succeed, making them dynamic and goal-oriented individuals.

At their core, Psychic Number 3 individuals possess an innate charm that draws people towards them. Their self-assured demeanour and natural eloquence make them effective communicators and influencers. Driven by a desire for recognition and success, they navigate life with a clear purpose, seeking out opportunities to shine on both personal and professional fronts. Strengths of Psychic Number 3 individuals lie in their unwavering determination and adaptability. They thrive in situations that require quick thinking and the ability to navigate diverse environments. Their confidence enables them to take risks and embrace challenges with enthusiasm, often inspiring others to follow their lead.

However, the pursuit of success can sometimes lead Psychic Number 3 individuals to become overly focused on external validation. Their desire for recognition might overshadow their authentic selves, causing them to lose sight of their intrinsic worth. This relentless pursuit of achievements may also result in burnout if not balanced with self-care. In careers, Psychic Number 3 individuals excel in roles that demand leadership, sales, public speaking, and roles that involve networking and social engagement. Their charismatic presence and goal-driven approach make them successful entrepreneurs, motivational speakers, politicians, and performers. In relationships, Psychic

Number 3 individuals seek partners who appreciate their drive and ambition while also encouraging them to stay grounded. They are attracted to individuals who support their goals and understand the demands of their busy lifestyles.

Their destiny revolves around embracing their role as achievers and influencers, using their charisma and determination to make a mark in their chosen endeavours. Psychic Number 3 embodies the archetype of the go-getter and motivator. Their dynamic presence and unrelenting pursuit of success empower them to inspire change and uplift those around them, leaving a lasting impact on the world.

The Psychic Number 4 signifies individuals who radiate creativity, depth, and an innate connection to emotions. Just as the number four signifies stability, these individuals possess a unique ability to ground themselves in their emotions, often expressing themselves through artistic and introspective means. Psychic Number 4 is associated with qualities of introspection, sensitivity, and a profound desire for meaning, making them profound and contemplative souls.

At their core, Psychic Number 4 individuals possess a deep well of emotions, often using creative outlets to express their inner world. Their introspective nature allows them to explore their thoughts and feelings, leading to a unique perspective that sets them apart. Driven by a need for authenticity and personal significance, they navigate life with a focus on finding deeper meaning in their experiences. Strengths of Psychic Number 4 individuals lie in their creative prowess and ability to connect emotionally with others. They excel at capturing emotions and translating them into various forms of art, be it visual, literary, or performing arts. Their contemplative nature allows them to explore the intricacies of life, offering insights that resonate with those around them.

However, the pursuit of authenticity can sometimes lead Psychic Number 4 individuals to experience bouts of melancholy or self-doubt. Their deep emotions may result in periods of introspection that can feel overwhelming, requiring them to find a balance between exploring their inner world and engaging with the external one. In careers, Psychic Number 4 individuals shine in roles that involve artistic expression, writing, counselling, and fields that require deep emotional connection. Their creative nature makes them excellent artists, writers, therapists, and spiritual guides. They have a unique ability to create works that evoke profound emotions and resonate with others on a soulful level. In relationships, Psychic Number 4 individuals seek partners who appreciate their depth, creativity, and emotional sensitivity. They are drawn to individuals who can engage in meaningful conversations and share their passion for exploring life's mysteries.

Their destiny revolves around embracing their role as creatives and introspective thinkers, using their unique perspective to inspire and touch the hearts of others. Psychic Number 4 embodies the archetype of the artist and philosopher. Their profound connection to emotions and authenticity empowers them to leave a lasting impact through their creative expressions and insights.

The Psychic Number 5 represents individuals who exude curiosity, analytical prowess, and a natural inclination for exploration. Just as the number five signifies change and versatility, these individuals are characterized by their insatiable thirst for knowledge and their ability to adapt to a variety of situations. Psychic Number 5 is associated with qualities of intellect, independence, and a strong desire to understand the world, making them perceptive and inquisitive minds.

At their core, Psychic Number 5 individuals possess an unquenchable curiosity that drives them to seek answers and unravel the mysteries of life. Their analytical nature allows them to delve deep into subjects, often becoming experts in their chosen fields. Driven by a need for intellectual freedom, they navigate life with a focus on expanding their knowledge and understanding. Strengths of Psychic Number 5 individuals lie in their sharp intellect and capacity for independent thinking. They excel at analysing complex situations and finding innovative solutions. Their ability to absorb information and make connections enables them to navigate various challenges with ease, often serving as reliable problem solvers.

However, the pursuit of knowledge can sometimes lead Psychic Number 5 individuals to become isolated or detached from emotions. Their emphasis on independence might make it challenging for them to fully engage in social interactions or express their feelings. In careers, Psychic Number 5 individuals thrive in roles that require research, analysis, and critical thinking. They excel in scientific fields, academia, technology, and positions that demand a deep understanding of complex systems. Their analytical approach and adaptability make them excellent researchers, scientists, engineers, and inventors. In relationships, Psychic Number 5 individuals seek partners who appreciate their intellect, independence, and capacity for deep thinking. They are drawn to individuals who engage them in intellectual conversations and provide the space they need to explore their interests.

Their destiny revolves around embracing their role as seekers of knowledge and pioneers of innovation, using their analytical prowess to make meaningful contributions. Psychic Number 5 embodies the archetype of the thinker and innovator. Their insatiable curiosity and ability to adapt empower them to leave a lasting impact by unravelling the complexities of the world and contributing to progress and understanding.

The Psychic Number 6 signifies individuals who radiate responsibility, loyalty, and a natural inclination to provide support and security. Just as the number six signifies stability, these individuals often play the role of caregivers and protectors, creating a safe and nurturing environment for those around them. Psychic Number 6 is associated with qualities of reliability, dedication, and a strong sense of duty, making them dependable and compassionate souls.

At their core, Psychic Number 6 individuals possess an unwavering sense of responsibility towards their loved ones and their community. Their loyalty and commitment run deep, often leading them to be the pillars of support in times of need. Driven by a need to create a secure foundation, they navigate life with a focus on ensuring the well-being of those they care for. Strengths of Psychic Number 6 individuals lie in their reliability and dedication. They excel at creating safe and harmonious environments, offering unwavering support to those around them. Their ability to anticipate and address potential challenges makes them valuable problem solvers and confidants.

However, the pursuit of security can sometimes lead Psychic Number 6 individuals to become anxious or overly cautious. Their need to protect and provide might cause them to worry excessively, especially in situations where they perceive potential threats. In careers, Psychic Number 6 individuals thrive in roles that involve caregiving, counselling, social work, and fields that require dedication to the well-being of others. Their compassionate nature makes them excellent nurses, therapists, teachers, and community organizers. They have a unique ability to create spaces where individuals feel safe and supported. In relationships, Psychic Number 6 individuals seek partners who appreciate their loyalty, support, and commitment. They are drawn to individuals who value their need for security and reciprocate their efforts to create a stable and harmonious relationship.

Their destiny revolves around embracing their role as protectors and caregivers, using their loyalty and dedication to foster a sense of security for themselves and those around them. Psychic Number 6 embodies the archetype of the nurturer and protector. Their unwavering commitment and compassionate nature empower them to leave a lasting impact by creating a safe haven and fostering connections based on trust and support.

The Psychic Number 7 characterises individuals who radiate enthusiasm, curiosity, and a natural inclination for exploration. Just as the number seven signifies spiritual growth and introspection, these individuals possess an insatiable curiosity and a thirst for uncovering life's mysteries. Psychic Number 7 is associated with qualities of optimism, creativity, and a strong desire for experiencing new adventures, making them adventurous and free-spirited souls.

At their core, Psychic Number 7 individuals possess an innate sense of wonder that drives them to seek diverse experiences and expand their horizons. Their optimistic outlook allows them to find joy in life's little pleasures, often inspiring others to embrace a similar perspective. Driven by a need for personal freedom, they navigate life with a focus on exploring the world around them and savouring the beauty it offers. Strengths of Psychic Number 7 individuals lie in their boundless enthusiasm and creative thinking. They excel at finding innovative solutions and thinking outside the box. Their ability to see the silver lining in any situation enables them to uplift others and infuse a sense of positivity into their surroundings.

However, the pursuit of excitement can sometimes lead Psychic Number 7 individuals to become easily distracted or scattered in their pursuits. Their desire for constant stimulation might make it challenging for them to stick to long-term commitments or fully engage in tasks that require sustained focus. In careers, Psychic Number 7 individuals thrive in roles that involve creativity, exploration, and a sense of adventure. They excel in fields related to travel, entertainment, arts, and positions that require innovative thinking. Their ability to infuse enthusiasm into their work makes them successful performers, artists, writers, and explorers. In relationships, Psychic Number 7 individuals seek partners who share their sense of adventure and curiosity. They are drawn to individuals who appreciate their free-spirited nature and encourage them to explore new horizons.

Their destiny revolves around embracing their role as adventurers and visionaries, using their optimism and creative energy to inspire and uplift those around them. Psychic Number 7 embodies the archetype of the explorer and dreamer. Their insatiable curiosity and ability to find joy in life empower them to leave a lasting impact by encouraging others to embrace life's adventures and possibilities.

The Psychic Number 8 signifies individuals who radiate power, authority, and a natural inclination for leadership. Just as the number eight signifies abundance and strength, these individuals possess a strong desire for control and the ability to navigate challenges with resilience. Psychic Number 8 is associated with qualities of determination, confidence, and a strong drive for success, making them assertive and influential souls.

At their core, Psychic Number 8 individuals possess an unwavering determination that propels them to overcome obstacles and achieve their goals. Their confidence and assertiveness command respect and authority, often leading them to take charge in various situations. Driven by a need for control and impact, they navigate life with a focus on achieving success and wielding their influence. Strengths of Psychic Number 8 individuals lie in their leadership skills and ability to make tough decisions. They excel at managing challenging situations and motivating others to work towards common goals. Their sense of responsibility and drive enable them to leave a lasting impact on their endeavours.

However, the pursuit of control can sometimes lead Psychic Number 8 individuals to become overly dominating or stubborn. Their strong-willed nature might make it challenging for them to delegate or consider alternative perspectives. In careers, Psychic Number 8 individuals thrive in roles that involve leadership, management, and positions of authority. They excel as entrepreneurs, executives, politicians, and leaders in various fields. Their assertive demeanour and ability to take charge make them effective in roles where making impactful decisions is crucial. In relationships, Psychic Number 8 individuals seek partners who appreciate their strength and ambition. They are drawn to individuals who can match their assertiveness and respect their need for independence.

Their destiny revolves around embracing their role as leaders and influencers, using their determination and authority to create positive change. Psychic Number 8 embodies the archetype of the achiever and trailblazer. Their unwavering determination and ability to navigate challenges empower them to leave a lasting impact by driving progress and inspiring others to reach their full potential.

The Psychic Number 9 characterizes individuals who exude compassion, harmony, and a natural inclination towards unity. Just as the number nine signifies completion and wholeness, these individuals possess a deep sense of empathy and a desire to create a harmonious environment for everyone. Psychic Number 9 is associated with qualities of patience, understanding, and a strong drive for peace, making them gentle and caring souls.

At their core, Psychic Number 9 individuals possess an innate ability to understand and connect with the emotions of others. Their patient and compassionate nature allows them to be a source of comfort and support, often playing the role of peacemakers. Driven by a need for balance and harmony, they navigate life with a focus on fostering a sense of unity and goodwill. Strengths of Psychic Number 9 individuals lie in their ability to create a sense of calm and bring people together. They excel at mediating conflicts and offering solace to those in need. Their understanding and patient approach enable them to nurture relationships and create spaces of acceptance.

However, the pursuit of harmony can sometimes lead Psychic Number 9 individuals to become overly accommodating or passive. Their desire to avoid conflicts might make it challenging for them to assert their own needs or make decisions that prioritize their well-being. In careers, Psychic Number 9 individuals thrive in roles that involve caregiving, counselling, and positions that require a nurturing presence. They excel as therapists, social workers, teachers, and in fields where empathy and understanding are essential. Their ability to create safe spaces makes them effective in roles that promote healing and connection. In relationships, Psychic Number 9 individuals seek partners who appreciate their compassion and respect their need for balance. They are drawn to individuals who share their values of unity and empathy.

Their destiny revolves around embracing their role as healers and peacemakers, using their compassion and harmony-seeking nature to create positive change. Psychic Number 9 embodies the archetype of the empath and harmonizer. Their ability to foster unity and offer support empowers them to leave a lasting impact by nurturing relationships and promoting understanding among individuals.

Destiny Number and Name Number

Once you've understood the traits associated with a Psychic Number, say it's Number 1 which often stands for leadership and a strong sense of independence, you've essentially cracked the code for the Destiny and Name Numbers if they're the same. Your Destiny Number, if also a 1, will use those traits of leadership to shape your larger life story—like what career you'll settle into, the kind of partner you'll have, and the overall direction your life will take, especially as you grow older. On the flip side, if your Name Number is 1, that leadership vibe gets broadcasted as your public persona. Whether it's in a job interview or just being the go-to person in a group of friends, you're stamped as someone who leads. So, the essence remains the same across Psychic, Destiny, and Name Numbers when they align. The difference lies in where these traits get to play their role: in your day-to-day reactions (Psychic Number), in your long-term life journey (Destiny Number), or in the way people first perceive you (Name Number). If you've grasped the core traits of your Psychic Number, you're already ahead of the curve in knowing how these traits are going to influence you in different areas when seen as your Destiny or Name Number.

Chapter Seventeen

The Contrast

How the Enneagram contrasts with numerology

The quest to understand the human psyche has fascinated scholars, mystics, and ordinary people alike. Various systems have been developed over the ages to decode the enigma that is human behaviour. Among these, the Enneagram, Vedic Numerology, and Chaldean Numerology are particularly noteworthy. All of them offer different perspectives and approaches, yet aim to achieve a common goal: understanding the person's inner world. Let's delve deeper into the intricacies of these systems, seeking to understand their origins, their methodologies, and what they reveal about us.

The Origin and Philosophical Backdrop

The Enneagram has roots in both spiritual traditions and modern psychology. It's like an amalgamation of age-old wisdom and new-age psychological theories. When you think of Enneagram, think of a system that explores the depths of human emotions, motivations, and fears. It is an evolved, comprehensive tool used globally for personal development and understanding human dynamics.

Vedic Numerology, on the other hand, springs from the ancient Indian culture steeped in astrology and spirituality. In this system, numbers are not just digits; they are carriers of vibrational energies. These vibrations are thought to be influenced by planets and other celestial bodies, painting a cosmic picture of a person's nature and destiny.

Chaldean Numerology also traces its roots back to ancient civilizations, particularly Babylon. Though it also regards numbers as carriers of energy, its focus is more on the mystical aspects of these numbers, rather than planetary influences. Here, numbers are not just digits; they're seen as entities possessing a kind of mystical energy that can influence your life.

Classification of Personalities and Complexity Levels

The Enneagram goes all out with its classification. With nine primary types and each type having subtypes and "wings" or adjacent types that influence it, the system provides a multi-layered look into human psychology. The classifications extend into more complex delineations like 'stress' and 'security' points, making it a nuanced tool for understanding human behaviour. In contrast, both Vedic and Chaldean Numerology have a simpler approach. Vedic Numerology focuses on numbers 1-9, associating each number with specific planetary influences. Chaldean Numerology employs numbers 1-8, and like its Vedic counterpart, every number represents certain characteristics and tendencies. The focus here is not on sub-categories but on the potency of each number itself.

Areas of Human Exploration

What's intriguing about all these systems is their shared commitment to fostering self-awareness. The Enneagram dissects human motivations, fears, and desires, illuminating how individuals respond to challenges and handle relationships. It not only explains but often predicts human responses to various life situations. The Enneagram, while primarily rooted in psychological theories, also provides a framework for personal growth. It suggests paths towards self-improvement and how one could evolve to higher levels of consciousness and self-actualization.

Vedic and Chaldean Numerology, however, take a somewhat different route. While they also delve into personality traits and characteristics, their approach is more cosmological or mystical. These systems aim to show how celestial or mystical energies influence human behaviour. They can point you toward understanding why you're inclined to make certain choices and how you can balance your traits for a better life. Going beyond mere personality traits, Vedic Numerology sometimes serves as a compass pointing towards one's life path and even destiny. Many practitioners believe that understanding your numbers can provide insights into your life's greater purpose. Chaldean Numerology, on the other hand, doesn't explicitly delve into the concept of life paths or destiny. It mostly confines itself to explaining traits and tendencies.

The contrast of numbers

Type 1: The Reformer vs Number 1: Sun - Enneagram Type 1, known as "The Reformer", is marked by an unwavering drive for perfection and a strong moral compass. These individuals tirelessly strive for self-improvement and the betterment of their surroundings. On the other hand, in Vedic numerology, Number 1 resonates with attributes of leadership, independence, and originality. While both systems underscore the significance of self-improvement, they diverge in their emphasis and nuances.

In Vedic numerology, individuals aligned with Number 1, like Mukesh Ambani and Carlos Slim Helu, exhibit a commanding presence as leaders and innovators. Their journeys reflect the pioneering spirit associated with Vedic Number 1, which extends beyond mere self-correction to embrace transformative innovation and fresh beginnings. As No. 1 entities, they embody qualities of individualism and originality that drive them to reach unparalleled heights.

The contrasting perspective emerges when examining Enneagram Type 1, where the focal point revolves around rectitude and adherence to principles. Figures like Nelson Mandela and Michelle Obama epitomize this trait, tirelessly advocating for justice and social change. While both systems acknowledge the pursuit of excellence, the Enneagram dives deeper into the realm of moral righteousness and ethical standards.

As we delve into the distinctive paths of Enneagram Type 1 and Vedic Numerology Number 1, one emphasizes the pursuit of moral perfection and self-improvement, the other showcases the dynamic essence of leadership and innovation. These contrasting yet complementary frameworks invite us to explore the multifaceted nature of human identity.

Type 2: The Helper vs Number 2: Moon - Enneagram Type 2 individuals, often referred to as "The Helper", radiate a selfless and nurturing nature, driven by a profound desire to support and care for others. In stark contrast, Vedic Numerology's Number 2 resonates with qualities of harmony, cooperation, and sensitivity. While both systems accentuate the significance of human connections, they diverge in their perspectives on giving and fostering empathetic bonds.

As we delve into the complexities of Type 2 personalities, a profound need to prioritize the needs of others over their own becomes evident. This intrinsic drive is entwined with a yearning for approval and likability. Similarly, luminaries such as Dolly Parton and Maya Angelou, who embody Vedic Number 2, emanate a harmonious energy that cultivates cooperative relationships and empathetic interactions. The crux of the contrast emerges in the intrinsic motivation of "The Helper" versus the quintessence of Vedic Number 2. The Enneagram delves into the intricate dynamics of self-sacrifice and altruism, often fuelled by the quest for affirmation. On the other hand, Vedic Number 2 encompasses a broader spectrum of cooperation and sensitivity, placing emphasis on the art of partnership and fostering empathetic connections.

The fusion of enigmatic personalities representative of Enneagram Type 2, exemplifies their nurturing and generous inclinations. Simultaneously, emblematic of Vedic Number 2, radiate qualities of diplomacy and empathy, acting as catalysts for bridges of understanding and harmonious collaboration.

The Contrast

As we explore the distinctive narratives of Enneagram Type 2 and Vedic Numerology Number 2, one archetype centres on selfless aid and the quest for approval, the other illuminates the beauty of empathy, cooperation, and the art of creating harmonious relationships.

Type 3: The Achiever vs Number 3: Jupiter - Enneagram Type 3 individuals, famously known as "The Achiever", are propelled by a relentless pursuit of success and recognition. They strive to achieve their goals while presenting a polished image. Vedic Numerology's Number 3, in contrast, embodies qualities of creativity, communication, and expression. As we delve into the dynamics of these archetypes, we uncover both their shared facets and distinct perspectives on achievement and self-expression.

The journey of the Achiever archetype is marked by an unwavering ambition to achieve excellence and garner affirmation. This compelling drive is often interwoven with a yearning for recognition and worthiness. Parallelly, luminaries symbolizing Vedic Number 3, exude an innate spark of creativity and a powerful ability to communicate through their respective fields.

The contrast materializes in the nuances of motivation: the Enneagram Type 3's pursuit of success and recognition versus the essence of Vedic Number 3, which encompasses the realms of creative expression and effective communication. The Achiever's dedication to showcasing competence aligns with the expansive energy of Jupiter, symbolizing wisdom and growth in Vedic numerology. However, the Vedic Number 3 extends beyond personal success to embrace the art of self-expression in myriad forms, including artistic, intellectual, and spiritual dimensions.

Type 4: The Individualist vs Number 4: Rahu - Enneagram Type 4 individuals, recognized as "The Individualist", are marked by their quest for authenticity and a longing for uniqueness. Intensely emotional and driven to find their true identity, they seek a deeper sense of self. In the realm of Vedic numerology, Number 4 embodies stability, practicality, and organization. As we delve into the essence of these archetypes, we unveil both their shared aspects and divergent perspectives on individuality and stability.

Decoding You

Within the narrative of the Individualist archetype lies a yearning to unravel their distinct identity. This journey is often intertwined with a profound sense of inner turmoil and an intricate relationship with shame. The concept of being an "outsider looking in" resonates strongly, reflecting their desire to be seen for their authentic selves. Parallelly, luminaries symbolic of Vedic Number 4, radiate a sense of stability and groundedness, paired with an ability to channel their emotions into creative expression.

The contrast between these archetypes manifests in the nature of identity exploration: the Enneagram Type 4's quest for authenticity and emotional depth versus the essence of Vedic Number 4, which signifies stability and practicality. The Individualist's emotional journey aligns with the transformative energy of Rahu, signifying a pursuit of unique experiences and self-discovery. While both systems acknowledge the importance of identity, Vedic Number 4 introduces a practical and structured approach to life's challenges.

Type 5: The Investigator vs Number 5: Mercury - Enneagram Type 5 individuals, known as "The Investigator", are driven by a quest for knowledge and a thirst for understanding complex concepts. They often retreat into their minds to explore the intricacies of the world around them. In the realm of Vedic numerology, Number 5 resonates with adaptability, versatility, and curiosity. As we delve into the essence of these archetypes, we discover their shared traits and distinct perspectives on knowledge and adaptability.

The Investigator archetype embodies an insatiable curiosity and an inclination to observe and analyse their surroundings. Their affinity for infinite possibility parallels Vedic Number 5's attributes of adaptability and curiosity. This shared pursuit of understanding aligns with both systems, underscoring the importance of knowledge in shaping their experiences.

In the Investigator's exploration of knowledge, luminaries like Albert Einstein and Stephen Hawking stand as exemplars of the Enneagram Type 5. Their relentless pursuit of scientific understanding and ground-breaking concepts mirror the adaptability and curiosity of Mercury's influence in Vedic numerology. This juxtaposition highlights the Investigator's intellectual curiosity and introversion, as well as their adaptability to shifting paradigms.

The contrast between these archetypes emerges in the nature of knowledge-seeking: the Enneagram Type 5's retreat into their minds for intellectual exploration versus Vedic Number 5's broader emphasis on adaptability and versatility. While the Investigator delves into complex concepts, the essence of Vedic Number 5 incorporates a multifaceted approach to understanding the world.

Type 6: The Loyalist vs Number 6: Venus - In the Enneagram world, Type 6 individuals are known as "The Loyalists", driven by a deep need for security and stability. They value loyalty and seek to establish a sense of safety in their relationships. In the realm of Vedic numerology, Number 6 resonates with attributes of responsibility, balance, and harmony. Both systems delve into the facets of loyalty and responsibility, while their nuanced perspectives offer insights into how these qualities manifest.

The Loyalist's commitment to security and the well-being of their loved ones aligns with Vedic Number 6's representation of responsibility and balance. This resonates with Vedic Number 6's emphasis on harmony and the need to strike a balance in all aspects of life. As we explore luminaries like Princess Diana and Tom Hanks within the Enneagram Type 6, we witness their embodiment of loyalty and their role as stabilizing forces in their spheres. This parallels Vedic Number 6's attribute of harmony, emphasizing their roles as harmonizers and peacemakers. Princess Diana's dedication to humanitarian causes and Tom Hanks' enduring reputation as a dependable actor mirror the essence of Vedic Number 6.

Contrastingly, the contrast arises in the nature of loyalty and responsibility: the Enneagram Type 6's emphasis on security in relationships versus Vedic Number 6's broader focus on maintaining balance and harmony in various aspects of life. The Loyalist's hesitancy to commit, as seen in Betsy Miller's experience, reflects the intricate dance between their need for security and the desire to strike a harmonious equilibrium. When we observe luminaries like Dr. APJ Abdul Kalam and Michael Jackson within Vedic

Number 6, we recognize the embodiment of harmony and responsibility in their distinct ways. Dr. Kalam's role as a visionary and leader aligns with Vedic Number 6's sense of balance, while Michael Jackson's creative expression and philanthropic endeavours echo the harmonious essence of this number.

Type 7: The Enthusiast vs Number 7: Ketu - Enneagram Type 7 individuals are often referred to as "The Enthusiasts", driven by a pursuit of excitement, new experiences, and avoiding pain. They thrive on a sense of adventure and the thrill of discovery. In the realm of Vedic numerology, Number 7 resonates with attributes of spirituality, intuition, and introspection. Both systems delve into the realm of curiosity and exploration, albeit from different perspectives.

The Enthusiast's boundless energy and love for novel experiences align with Vedic Number 7's representation of spirituality and intuition. Alli Worthington's journey of using her struggles to inspire her creative work reflects the Enthusiast's desire for personal growth and sharing life lessons. This resonates with Vedic Number 7's emphasis on spiritual exploration and seeking deeper truths. As we delve into luminaries within the Enneagram Type 7, we witness their embodiment of enthusiasm and their ability to bring joy to others. This mirrors Vedic Number 7's attribute of intuition, reflecting the Enthusiast's ability to tap into their inner wisdom and creative expression. The contrast emerges in the nature of curiosity and exploration: the Enneagram Type 7's pursuit of exciting experiences versus Vedic Number 7's emphasis on spiritual insights and intuitive understanding. The Enthusiast's energetic pursuit of happiness contrasts with Vedic Number 7's introspective and spiritually oriented perspective.

Type 8: The Challenger vs Number 8: Saturn - Enneagram Type 8 individuals, known as "The Challengers", are driven by a need for control, power, and autonomy. They assert themselves and take charge of situations. In Vedic numerology, Number 8 resonates with ambition, authority, and material success. While both systems emphasize attributes of strength and authority, they differ in their approaches to control and achievement.

The Challenger's strong desire for control and assertion aligns with Vedic Number 8's attributes of ambition and authority and drive to achieve their goals and assert their influence. This parallels Vedic Number 8's focus on material success and the pursuit of leadership.

Notable figures like Martin Luther King Jr. and Bernie Sanders exhibit qualities of both the Challenger and Vedic Number 8. Martin Luther King Jr.'s unwavering advocacy for civil rights resonates with the Challenger's determination to make a difference, while also aligning with Vedic Number 8's emphasis on leadership and authority. Similarly, Bernie Sanders' passionate pursuit of social justice reflects the Challenger's assertiveness and Vedic Number 8's ambition. The contrast becomes apparent in their approaches to control and power. While the Challenger seeks control through assertion, Vedic Number 8's pursuit of ambition extends to material success and authority.

In the realm of achievement and authority, the Vedic Number 8 encompasses a broader spectrum, including material and societal success. Figures like Guru Nanak and JRD Tata represent the attributes of Vedic Number 8: ambition, authority, and accomplishment. Guru Nanak's founding of Sikhism and JRD Tata's contributions to industry exemplify Vedic Number 8's focus on leadership and material achievement.

Type 9: The Peacemaker vs Number 9: Mars - Enneagram Type 9 individuals, known as "The Peacemakers", are characterized by their desire for harmony, avoidance of conflict, and tendency to merge with others. They seek unity and strive to maintain inner and outer peace. In Vedic numerology, Number 9 signifies humanitarianism, compassion, and service. While both systems acknowledge the importance of harmony, they diverge in the way they approach unity and action.

The Peacemaker's inclination toward avoiding conflict and maintaining peace resonates with Vedic Number 9's attributes of compassion and service. Amanda Sudano's description of her harmonious relationship with her husband reflects the Peacemaker's natural tendency to create unity. This aligns with Vedic Number 9's emphasis on humanitarianism and a desire to serve the greater good.

The contrast arises in the realm of action and assertiveness: the Peacemaker's inclination toward merging and avoiding conflict versus Vedic Number 9's emphasis on compassionate service. Seth Abrams' experience of dispersing himself to maintain peace underscores the Peacemaker's tendency to adapt and avoid confrontation.

The Final Word

In summary, these three systems offer rich, multi-layered approaches to understanding human personality and behaviour. The Enneagram, with its complex psychological profiles, provides a detailed map of the human psyche. Vedic and Chaldean Numerology, with their simpler yet profound emphasis on numbers, offer an alternative route to self-discovery that is equally captivating. Despite their divergent origins and approaches, they all contribute to the mosaic of tools we can use to better understand ourselves and the people around us. By investing time in understanding each of these systems, we can attain a more holistic self-understanding that enriches our life journey.

***

Chapter Eighteen

The Unfinished Symphony

Before you head out to the sea...

As we conclude our journey through the fascinating realms of Enneagram and Vedic numerology, we find ourselves equipped with profound tools that extend far beyond the boundaries of mere personality analysis. These systems offer not only insights into our own characteristics but also a window into understanding the dynamics of our relationships and the intricate web of human interaction.

Through the Enneagram, we gain the invaluable ability to peer into the intricate architecture of our inner motivations, fears, and desires. This newfound self-awareness not only empowers us to embrace our strengths but also confront our vulnerabilities, leading to a journey of personal growth and transformation. The Enneagram serves as a mirror that reflects our true selves, allowing us to foster healthier relationships by understanding our reactions and responses to others.

The Enneagram is a powerful tool for discovering who we are and improving ourselves. Unlike some other personality systems, it's not fixed – it encourages us to keep exploring our traits and motivations as we grow. The Enneagram suggests that our main personality type comes from specific fears or motivations, which shape how we act and see the world. This insight can help us become better versions of ourselves. When we figure out our

Enneagram type, we learn about our usual patterns – what we're good at and where we struggle. This self-awareness becomes a base for personal growth. We can use our strengths while also working on our weaknesses. The Enneagram talks about different levels of development for each type, showing us how to become emotionally and mentally healthier. This helps us have better relationships, accept ourselves more, and feel happier overall.

The Enneagram also teaches us that all nine types are connected. Knowing that each type has its own fears and motivations makes it easier to get along with others. This can be really useful at work when we need to work well with others. The Enneagram also talks about wings, arrows, and paths of integration. These are fancy terms, but they're simple concepts.

Wings mean we can learn from the types next to ours. Arrows show how we act under stress or when we're growing. Paths of integration guide us on how to handle challenges and make the most of opportunities. Famous psychologists like Carl Jung believed that knowing ourselves is key to growing as a person. The Enneagram agrees with this idea. It's like a roadmap for exploring our minds and hearts. When we combine Enneagram ideas with psychological concepts, we have a strong toolkit for self-improvement. The Enneagram is a flexible way to learn about ourselves and get better. It encourages us to dig into our traits and motivations. With self-awareness, understanding others, and using smart strategies, the Enneagram helps us improve our relationships, happiness, and well-being.

Simultaneously, Vedic numerology unveils the cosmic energies that influence our lives and destinies. By delving into the vibrations of our numerological numbers, we unlock a deeper understanding of our inherent qualities and potentials. Armed with this knowledge, we can harness our strengths to steer our careers, relationships, and personal endeavours towards fulfilment and success. The intersection of these two systems magnifies their impact. By combining the Enneagram's exploration of inner motivations with Vedic numerology's cosmic insights, we create a comprehensive roadmap for enhancing our lives. We learn to appreciate the uniqueness of both ourselves and others, leading to improved relationships based on empathy, understanding, and acceptance. It's important to note that the glimpse we've shared in this book is just the tip of the iceberg. Both Enneagram and Vedic numerology are vast and intricate fields of study, each containing layers of wisdom waiting to be explored. The first taste we've provided is merely an invitation to embark on a lifelong journey of self-discovery, relationship enhancement, and personal growth.

Absolutely, the journey of mastering the Enneagram and Vedic numerology is akin to savouring a delectable cuisine that requires time, patience, and a continuous quest for deeper understanding. Just as a seasoned chef refines their skills through years of experimentation and learning from other culinary experts, so too must we approach these systems with an open heart and a willingness to learn from both experts and our own observations.

The paths of self-discovery and personal growth are never static; they are dynamic and ever-evolving. The wisdom offered by the Enneagram and Vedic numerology is not confined to the pages of a book but rather flows through the fabric of our lives, constantly shaping and enriching our experiences. Each interaction, each introspection, and each insight is a stepping stone on this transformative journey. Just as a seasoned traveller gains deeper insights into different cultures and landscapes over time, the same applies to our journey with these systems. We learn to read the intricate map of our own psyche and decode the cosmic energies that guide us. Along the way, we not only unravel the mysteries of our inner world but also cultivate the ability to navigate relationships, make informed decisions in our careers, and approach life's challenges with wisdom and grace.

The Enneagram and numerology offer valuable tools for leadership development that can enhance a leader's effectiveness, self-awareness, and team connections. These systems bring different viewpoints that, when combined, create a well-rounded approach to improving leadership skills. The Enneagram focuses on personality types and motivations, helping leaders understand their leadership style's impact on their team. By discovering their Enneagram type, leaders can learn about their strengths and areas to improve. This self-awareness lets leaders use their strengths and work on their weaknesses. For example, a Type 1 leader (a "Reformer") might be great at ethics but could learn to delegate tasks more. By balancing strengths and areas to improve, leaders become more adaptable. Numerology introduces life path numbers and traits linked to numbers. Applying numerology to leadership can provide insight into leadership qualities. A leader with a life path number 1 might have traits like independence and confidence. Recognizing these traits lets leaders align their style with their natural tendencies, inspiring their team.

Combining Enneagram and numerology insights gives a better view of leadership. A Type 8 leader (a "Challenger") with a life path number 1 might have a bold leadership style. Knowing this, they can use their assertiveness for positive change while considering their team's needs. A Type 2 leader (a "Helper") with a life path number 6 might excel at building relationships and support, creating a caring work environment. Both systems stress growth.

Leaders can use them to check their progress, find areas to improve, and set goals. The Enneagram's levels of development and numerology's life cycles encourage lifelong self-improvement. Adding Enneagram and numerology to leadership programs makes development more personalized. By understanding motivations, inclinations, and challenges, leaders can adjust strategies for their team. This alignment improves communication, builds trust, and encourages teamwork. Overall, combining these systems empowers leaders to embrace their unique style while always growing and getting better.

At the core of effective leadership lies self-awareness. The Enneagram and numerology provide powerful tools for leaders to gain an in-depth understanding of their individual traits, strengths, and areas for growth. By recognizing their Enneagram type and life path number, leaders can align their leadership style with their innate qualities, resulting in a leadership approach characterized by authenticity and transparency. An essential aspect of successful team dynamics is understanding and collaboration. Through the integration of Enneagram and numerology insights, managers can customize their leadership strategies to accommodate the preferences and strengths of individual team members. This tailored approach cultivates an environment where each team member's distinct contributions are acknowledged and valued, leading to heightened team cohesion and productivity.

Conflict resolution and effective communication are pivotal skills for leaders. The Enneagram's categorization of personality types equips managers with insights into the underlying motivations and fears of team members, facilitating empathetic conflict resolution. In parallel, numerology offers insights into individuals' communication and conflict-resolution approaches based on their life path numbers. By combining these insights, managers can navigate conflicts with empathy, fostering healthy and respectful resolutions. Leadership development programs can benefit significantly from the integration of Enneagram and numerology insights. Workshops and coaching sessions centred on exploring one's Enneagram type and life path number enable leaders to delve into their decision-making processes, communication styles, and leadership strengths. This integration encourages continuous self-awareness and personal evolution, contributing to leaders' growth both personally and professionally.

Talent management and recruitment practices can be enhanced through the integration of these insights. By considering candidates' personality types and life path numbers in relation to team dynamics, organizations can assemble teams that are not only diverse but also compatible in terms of attributes and contributions. This approach fosters the creation of teams that can collectively achieve organizational success. The area of change management requires leaders to anticipate and navigate reactions to change within the organization. Enneagram and numerology insights enable managers to comprehend how personality types and life path numbers influence team members' perceptions and responses to change. Armed with this knowledge, managers can tailor communication strategies, support mechanisms, and incentives to facilitate a smooth transition and minimize resistance. Leadership coaching gains depth and efficacy when enriched with Enneagram and numerology insights. Coaches can utilize their clients' Enneagram types and life path numbers to guide leaders in making more effective decisions, resolving conflicts, and pursuing personal growth strategies. This personalized approach empowers leaders to harness their unique attributes for leadership excellence.

The integration of Enneagram and numerology insights into management practices introduces a transformative approach to leadership that emphasizes self-awareness, empathy, and individualization. By recognizing the rich diversity of human attributes and motivations, managers can foster an environment characterized by authentic leadership, effective communication, and collaborative team dynamics. Amidst the complexities of the modern business landscape, the wisdom embedded within the Enneagram and numerology equips leaders with the tools to navigate challenges, inspire their teams, and drive sustainable organizational growth.

In essence, this book serves as an introduction—a tantalizing taste of the boundless feast that awaits those who embark on the path of mastering the Enneagram and Vedic numerology. With each new discovery, each correction of understanding, and each connection forged between the systems and our lives, we move closer to the mastery that promises a life enriched with authenticity, purpose, and profound insights into both ourselves and the world around us.

So, as you continue your journey, embrace the challenge and the delight that comes with mastering these systems. Just as a chef's craft is refined over years of dedication, your understanding of the Enneagram and Vedic numerology will deepen over time, opening doors to a world of self-awareness, harmony, and meaningful connections. As you continue to explore these systems, remember that the insights you gain about yourself and others have the potential to reshape your interactions, your career trajectory, and your personal development. Through the synergy of the Enneagram and Vedic numerology, you hold the keys to a more fulfilling life—a life marked by authenticity, enriched relationships, and a profound understanding of the intricate tapestry of human existence.

ॐ पूर्णमदः पूर्णमिदं पूर्णात्पूर्णमुदच्यते ।
पूर्णस्य पूर्णमादाय पूर्णमेवावशिष्यते ॥
ॐ शान्तिः शान्तिः शान्तिः ॥

— *Ishavasya Upanishad*

Reference Section: Further Reading on the Enneagram

1. Riso, D.R. and Hudson, R. (1999). *The Wisdom of the Enneagram: The Complete Guide to Psychological and Spiritual Growth for the Nine Personality Types.* New York: Bantam Books.

2. Riso, D.R. and Hudson, R. (1987). *Personality Types: Using the Enneagram for Self-Discovery.* New York: Houghton Mifflin Harcourt.

3. Chestnut, B. (2013). *The Complete Enneagram: 27 Paths to Greater Self-Knowledge.* Berkeley: She Writes Press.

4. Palmer, H. (1995). *The Enneagram in Love and Work.* San Francisco: HarperCollins.

5. Palmer, H. (1991). *The Enneagram: Understanding Yourself and the Others in Your Life.* San Francisco: HarperSanFrancisco.

6. Riso, D.R. (1993). *Enneagram Transformations: Releases and Affirmations for Healing Your Personality Type.* Boston: Houghton Mifflin Harcourt.

7. Maitri, S. (2000). *The Spiritual Dimension of the Enneagram: Nine Faces of the Soul.* New York: TarcherPerigee.

8. Case, S. (2020). *The Honest Enneagram.* HarperOne.

9. Lagan, H.A. (2011). *Chaldean Numerology for Beginners: How Your Name and Birthday Reveal Your True Nature & Life Path.* Llewellyn Publications.

10. Thompson, L.B. (2019). *The Chaldean Numerology System.* Independent Publisher.

12. Johari, H. (1990). *Numerology With Tantra, Ayurveda, and Astrology.* Destiny Books.

13. Elinwood, E. (2006). *The Everything Numerology Book: Discover Your Potential for Love, Success, and Health Through the Science of Numbers.* Adams Media.

www.ingramcontent.com/pod-product-compliance
Lightning Source LLC
Chambersburg PA
CBHW020442110526
44587CB00038B/933